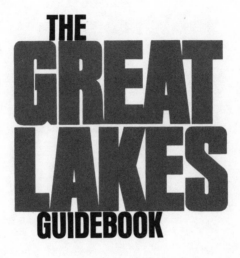

George Cantor

THE GREAT LAKES GUIDEBOOK

Lake Huron and Eastern Lake Michigan

Ann Arbor   The University of Michigan Press

In Canada: John Wiley & Sons Canada, Limited

Library of Congress Cataloging in Publication Data

Cantor, George, 1941–   (Revised)
  The Great Lakes guidebook.

  Bibliography: v. 1., p. 232; v. 2, p.
  CONTENTS: [1.] Lakes Ontario and Erie.—[2.] Lake
Huron and eastern Lake Michigan.   1.   Great Lakes
region—Description and travel—Guide-books.   I.   Title.
F551.C34   1977   917.7'04'3   77-13606
ISBN 0–472–19650–2 (v. 1)
ISBN 0–472–19651–0 (v. 2)

Contents

Maps

Introduction

Discovery is an attribute that seems to be disappearing from travel. Chain operations, interstate highways, and package tours all tend to reduce the travel experience to a set of predictable and orderly clichés. The unexpected is discouraged, the chance of surprise diminished. We now have the opportunity to go farther and faster than any people in history, only to find at journey's end that we really have not been anyplace at all.

There is even a booklet that tells travelers on Interstate 75 exactly where all the chain operations lie along the route. So one can drive from Sault Ste. Marie, Michigan, to Tampa, Florida, unhindered by anything resembling a local operation or with regional flavor. Aside from the fact that it snows a lot at the Soo and hardly ever at Tampa, the trip goes nowhere.

The research for these travel books has been fun for me. I have lived along the Great Lakes all my life. My family used to own summer cottages on Lake Erie and other summers have been spent on the shores of Lakes Huron and Michigan. I have traveled the region extensively, both professionally and aimlessly. I felt it could hold few surprises for me. I was wrong.

I don't know, for example, how many times I had driven past Goderich, Ontario, on the main road without ever stopping to see what the place looked like. This trip I did, and found one of the most delightful little towns I have ever seen. On other forays, I found a modern mining boomtown, an art colony, and a museum village of the Michigan lumbering era. They were all within a day's ride of my home, but somehow I had never seen them before and was only vaguely aware of their existence.

Before undertaking the research for this volume, I had not visited Mackinac Island in eighteen years. During that time I had been to Europe ten times and to forty-eight of the fifty states, but never back to this wonderful island just five hours from home. It was like rereading a book that had delighted you as a child and finding the wonder was still fresh.

In an earlier volume I wrote about Cleveland, Ohio, a city I had visited many times as a sportswriter. I thought then it was the dullest, most flavorless place in the country. I wrote sarcastically, at the time, that the only thing to do was stare out my hotel window and watch Lake Erie get polluted. But this time I looked at Cleveland as a potential tourist and what I saw astonished me. It had been there all the time, but I had never looked before.

So these Great Lakes books have been a voyage of discovery for me. Like thousands of others who live along their shores, I have taken the Lakes for granted. I had to be reminded that discovery is still there for those who look and that it can take place right down the road just as easily as across an ocean.

The Lakes are the perfect example of the wonder close at hand that we simply overlook. I know of few sights more thrilling than the lights of a giant freighter as it slips soundlessly past a great city at night. Or the first glimpse of blue water through the trees as the highway nears a lake. I am always surprised at how exciting that can be.

When I hear people who should know better complain about the dull scenery and lackluster history of the Midwest, and then learn that they have never been to Mackinac or Put-in-Bay, I am saddened. When I find that they have never stood on a Lake Superior bluff with the pines singing in the wind behind them, I am amused. There are landscapes of water, shore, and sky on the Lakes that compare favorably to any vista I have ever known. Yet there are those who will travel thousands of miles to take in scenery of approximate grandeur, return home full of snapshots and adjectives and never know what they're missing just a day's drive away. Or maybe they just have to be reminded. That is one purpose of this book.

Then there is the aftermath of the environmental awakening. The attention focused on the scandalous conditions in much of the Lakes system has resulted in stringent new pollution laws and controls. Miracles have been worked in the space of a decade. Some areas of the Lakes now enjoy cleaner water than at anytime in the last half century. Treatment plants are making a measurable impact on sewage and detergents dumped into the Lakes. (By the mid-70s, though, a new danger—concentrations of the chemical compound PCB, used in plastics and many other items—had been discovered in the Lakes' fish.) The patient is far from cured but the prognosis is improving. Except for a few trouble spots, the Upper Lakes are faring well. Ontario is described as holding its own by the international commission charged with overseeing the Lakes' environment. Even Erie, officially pronounced dead by the media during the height of the horror stories, has improved and may yet recover. But the initial publicity had a long-lasting effect. Once the public was alerted, it was hard to persuade people that the Lakes were improving. In areas removed from the Lakes, the Great Lakes were scratched off vacation lists and were never returned. Many travelers have not been back for years or have never seen the Lakes at all. This book is also meant for them.

Each of the five Great Lakes has its own personality, a set of characteristics that are apparent to those who sail their waters or who spend any length of time on their shores.

Lake Superior is the largest body of fresh water on the globe. It covers an area larger than the state of Maine, a total of 31,800 square miles. Its scenery matches its size. Superior is rimmed by hills and rugged bluffs, the most spectacular landscapes on the Lakes, and some of the grandest in the hemisphere. It is the *Gitche Gumee* of the Chippewas, the "laughing big sea water" of Longfellow's *Hiawatha*. But to the French it was *supérieur*. The bustling harbors at its western end—Duluth-

Superior and Thunder Bay—send the freighters away full of grain and ore, making the lake a vital segment in the economy of two nations. These ports, however, are the only cities of any size on Superior's shores. Its largest island is Isle Royale, a U.S. national park and wilderness preserve. Other major geographic features are the Apostle Islands, Wisconsin, now a national lakeshore; the Pictured Rocks, also a national lakeshore, in Michigan; and the long, hooked arm of the ruggedly beautiful Keewenaw Peninsula of Michigan. The lake empties into the St. Mary River at the twin cities of Sault Ste. Marie. The Soo Locks there carry twice the traffic of the Panama Canal.

STATISTICS OF THE GREAT LAKES

Lakes	Length mi. km.	Breadth mi. km.	Size sq. mi. km.^{2}	Greatest Depth ft. m.	Largest Cities
Superior	350	160	31,800	1,333	Thunder Bay, Ontario
	560	256	82,362	406	Duluth, Minnesota
					Superior, Wisconsin
Huron	206	183	23,010	750	Sarnia, Ontario
	330	293	59,595	229	Port Huron, Michigan
					Bay City, Michigan
Michigan	307	118	22,400	923	Chicago, Illinois
	491	189	58,016	281	Milwaukee, Wisconsin
					Gary, Indiana
Erie	241	57	9,910	210	Cleveland, Ohio
	386	91	25,667	64	Buffalo, New York
					Toledo, Ohio
Ontario	193	53	7,550	802	Toronto, Ontario
	309	85	19,555	244	Hamilton, Ontario
					Rochester, New York

Lake Huron comes next, the lake first seen by Europeans but the one that has remained least developed. Samuel de Champlain reached its shores in 1615. He had worked his way from Montreal along the Ottawa River, overland to Lake Nipissing and then along the French River to its outlet at the lake. He took this rather circuitous route west because the hostile Iroquois controlled the southern approaches. The existence of

Lakes Erie and Ontario was then only a vague rumor. Even with this head start, Huron has remained far off the main-traveled roads. The site at which Champlain first saw the lake remains inaccessible by automobile. Lake Huron's largest city, Sarnia, Ontario, has a population of about 60,000. The only other significant pocket of industry is concentrated on Saginaw Bay, which contributes whatever pollution the lake suffers. It is the second largest of the Lakes and the most irregularly shaped. Its massive eastern arm, Georgian Bay, is cut off from the rest of the lake by Manitoulin Island, the largest island on the Lakes. Other islands shield the North Channel. There are two units of Georgian Bay Islands National Park in Canada, one near Midland and the other at the tip of the slender Bruce Peninsula, near Tobermory. Mackinac Island, one of the stateliest resorts in the States, guards the western approach to Lake Huron at the Straits of Mackinac.

Lake Michigan is separated from Lake Huron only by a narrow strait. The two lakes lie at the same distance above sea level and are virtual twins in size. But Michigan is a lake with a split personality. At its southern end, unlike Huron, it supports one of the most intensive concentrations of industrial wealth and population in the world. Chicago, the pivotal metropolis of the Lakes, occupies its southwestern corner. The band of development continues eastward around the Calumet district of Indiana and northward to Milwaukee, another booming port and industrial center. But where the suburbs of the Wisconsin city end, the North begins and Lake Michigan becomes a resort-studded jewel. Its waves lap at some of the richest vacation property in the Midwest. Green Bay, on the Wisonsin shore, has the Door Peninsula, and on the east the two Traverse Bays, Great and Little, are lined with showplaces. Nearby is the Sleeping Bear Dunes National Lakeshore. Michigan is the only Great Lake entirely within the boundaries of the United States, but its largest island, Beaver, once was ruled by a king—albeit a self-proclaimed monarch.

The accumulated flows of Lakes Michigan and Huron empty into the St. Clair River at the cities of Sarnia and Port

Huron. At the far end they flow into Lake St. Clair, a sort of Great Lake, junior grade. At 460 square miles it is somewhat bigger than a pond but not in the same league as its enormous neighbors. Its Canadian shoreline is mostly undeveloped and Walpole Island is occupied by an Indian reservation. Detroit's suburbs sprawl along its southwestern end. At Belle Isle it meets the Detroit River, busiest inland waterway in the world and scene of industrialization beyond compare.

Lake Erie is the shallowest, busiest, oldest, and dirtiest of the Lakes. Sailors distrust it. The lake is shaped like a saucer and when storms come out of the west it can be a treacherous body of water. One of these gales can cause a thirteen-foot difference in water level at opposite ends of the lake and raise waves of frightening size. With an average depth of just fifty-eight feet Erie is also especially susceptible to industrial pollution and because of pollution it has suffered more severely than any other lake. Its southern shoreline is covered with major ports, from Toledo to Buffalo, while industrial discharges from Detroit almost succeeded in killing it. The lake is improving but is by no stretch of the imagination clean. Still, it supports major resort areas around Ohio's Sandusky Bay and the Presque Isle Peninsula of Pennsylvania. In contrast to the American shore, the Canadian side of Erie is almost empty, with only small resorts and fishing towns breaking the long stretches of solitude. Point Pelee and Long Point, both major wildlife sanctuaries and bird refuges, are the main landmarks. Pelee Island, largest in the lake, belongs to Canada and is primarily agricultural.

Erie empties into the churning Niagara River, which thunders over its escarpment a few miles on to form one of the world's great natural wonders. A few miles beyond Niagara Falls, the river passes through a tumultuous gorge before peacefully emerging into the last of the Lakes.

Lake Ontario is the least Great Lake, covering only 7,550 square miles, which is still a larger area than the state of New Jersey. But it is second deepest with an average sounding of 283 feet. Its depth results in a strong moderating influence over the adjacent countryside, and one of the great fruit belts of North

America is situated around its littoral. The western end of the lake is Ontario's most densely populated region. Toronto, second largest city in the country, and Hamilton, one of Canada's greatest manufacturing centers, present a solid belt of intensive development. On the American side, however, Rochester is the only city of significant size. The shoreline is quite regular, with only the mass of Quinte's Isle breaking into the lake from the north. There are no islands of any size in Lake Ontario, aside from the farthest eastern corner. There Wolfe and Amherst, Ontario, guard the entrance to the St. Lawrence River at Kingston, eastern limit to the Lakes.

From Duluth, Minnesota, to Kingston, Ontario, it has been a journey of 1,160 miles. We have passed through the world's largest freshwater system, the largest inland water transportation network—the superlatives go on and on. You might consider this. The Great Lakes' system contains sixty-seven trillion gallons of water and much of it is even drinkable.

In terms of geological time, the Great Lakes are rank upstarts. They began taking shape about 18,000 years ago, the end product of North America's final age of glacial activity. It was called the Wisconsin Age, because the ice reached to what is now the southern limits of that state. As the glaciers started their long retreat, ancient stream valleys were uncovered and slowly began filling with melt water and rain. Lakes formed in the area of Chicago and the Maumee Valley, both bodies of water draining into the Mississippi River. As the ice moved farther north the patterns changed. The lakes twisted into new shapes and sent their waters over newly formed drainage routes. Lake Erie and the southern portion of Lake Michigan had reached an approximation of their present forms about 10,000 years ago. Lake Ontario was shaped about 7,000 years ago. The Upper Lakes assumed their present outline a mere 3,000 years ago.

We have said previously that Champlain was the first European to see the Lakes, but that may not be strictly true. A shadowy figure named Etienne Brulé, sent out by Champlain to scout the area, may actually have reached the Lakes as early as 1612. It is hard to say. Brulé left no records. He was illiterate and was the first of the voyageurs to successfully adapt to the ways of the Indians. Eventually he was killed by them in the wilderness, after ranging from Lake Ontario to Isle Royale. He is, however, given credit for being the first European to see Lake Superior.

Twenty years after Champlain's expedition, Jean Nicolet explored Lake Michigan, reaching the site of Green Bay, Wisconsin. By 1631, two Jesuit priests, Fathers Jogues and Rambault, had established missions there and on Lake Superior, at Ashland, Wisconsin, and the Soo. Not until 1669 was the last of the Lakes discovered. Louis Joliet and Robert LaSalle entered Lake Erie a few days apart that summer from opposite directions. In another four years, Joliet and Father Marquette would discover the route from the Lakes to the Mississippi River and Fort Frontenac would be established as a permanent settlement at the mouth of the St. Lawrence River.

Finally, in 1679, LaSalle embarked on the crowning epic of Great Lakes discovery. Aboard his ship, the *Griffon,* he sailed across Erie, up the Detroit River and around Huron into Michigan, finally disembarking at Green Bay. The voyage opened up the southern route to the Upper Lakes and clarified the geographic relationship between the two segments. LaSalle went on to trace the Mississippi River to the Gulf of Mexico. The *Griffon* was sent home to Lake Erie and on the way back it vanished. Several museums around the Lakes display bits and pieces of what is thought to be the wreckage of the ship. But that is only guesswork. No one knows what happened to the ship or exactly where it went down. On that mysterious note the great discoveries on the Lakes ended and the age of settlement began.

It took the War of 1812 to establish the boundary between the United States and Canada in the Great Lakes area. In 1817 the border was settled by the Rush-Bagot Agreement and it has not been changed since.

Crossing this frontier is usually an uncomplicated, rapid procedure. No documents are required for citizens of either country, but it is advisable to carry some proof of citizenship, such as a copy of a birth certificate or voter registration card. Naturalized citizens should carry their certificates of naturalization and aliens must have their registration cards.

Motorists should have proof of car ownership and insurance coverage with them. Most personal items may cross the border without trouble, but rifles and expensive camera equipment should be registered at the border. No handguns are permitted in Canada.

Dogs may cross the border upon presentation of a certificate that the animal has been vaccinated against rabies in the last year. A description of the animal must accompany the certificate. Cats may cross freely.

For complete customs information, the traveler should request information, in advance, from the Customs Office in either Washington, D.C., or Ottawa, Ontario.

All of which brings us to this book.

It has been my experience as a travel editor that travel books fall roughly into two major categories. There are the personalized books of essays and observations, which may be great fun to read but not much help when it comes right down to planning a trip. Then there are the nuts-and-bolts sorts of listings, which have all the facts and figures but are about as readable as the Yellow Pages.

I have tried to stake out a middle ground. It is my hope that the essays in this book are written in a manner that will entertain. But I also intend for this book to be used as a planner and an on-the-road reference guide.

It is a selective guidebook. I have made no attempt to catalog every sight and attraction on the shoreline of the Great Lakes. I did endeavor, though, to list the best and most significant. They are the places that reflect the long and colorful history of the area, with appeal that is unique to the Lakes.

At the beginning of each chapter, there is an introductory essay about the particular area being explored. It will examine some of the features that influenced the area's historical development and the special qualities that can be found there.

Offered next are three attractions that I have selected as being the best in the area. If you are traveling through, these are the things you should make a special effort to see. Some of them are among the best-known sights on the continent, others are rarely publicized outside their immediate locale. But they are all top-notch attractions. These three sights are discussed in depth, and several are accompanied by useful maps.

After that follows a section we have called "Other Things to See." They are listed in about the order in which you would encounter them were you to drive across the area. A few of these sights are marked with bold-face numbers. This indicates that while they do not quite rank with the "Top Three" in the area, they are nonetheless unusually worthwhile and significant attractions. The others on the list can be seen during a stay of a few days in the area or may appeal to special interests. Other maps in this section have insets showing greater detail of the major cities in the area not otherwise visible in the larger map.

Then a section called "Side Trips," suggesting interesting things to see within a 50-mile drive of the lakeshore, is presented. Finally, there is a list of major state and provincial parks in the area, especially those with lakefront recreational facilities. If overnight camping is permitted, the number of tent sites is given.

That, in brief, is our book.

Read it and enjoy it. Most of all, use it.

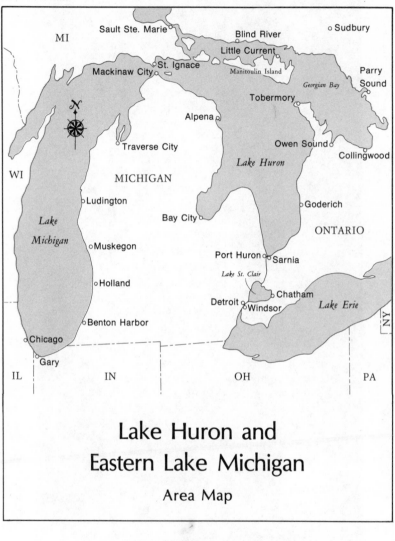

Sudbury

Sault Ste. Marie

MI

Blind River

Little Current

St. Ignace

Mackinaw City

Manitoulin Island

Parry
Sound

Georgian Bay

Tobermory

N

Alpena

Traverse City

Lake Huron

Owen Sound

Collingwood

MICHIGAN

Ludington

Bay City

Goderich

ONTARIO

WI

Lake
Michigan

Muskegon

Holland

Port Huron
Sarnia

Lake St. Clair

Chatham

Benton Harbor

Detroit
Windsor

Lake Erie

Chicago

NY

Gary

IL

IN

OH

PA

Lake Huron and
Eastern Lake Michigan

Area Map

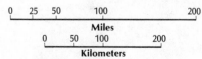

0   25   50   100   200
Miles

0   50   100   200
Kilometers

The Mackinac Bridge is a five-mile span connecting Michigan's Upper and Lower Peninsulas. *Courtesy Upper Michigan Tourist Association.*

1

The Straits of Mackinac

The history can be read in the names. The island is spelled Mackinac, the city is Mackinaw, and the bridge is the Mighty Mac. The same word, and yet very different. It illustrates, however, the one overriding fact about the area. From the first days of the European presence in North America to the present, Mackinac has been the great crossroads of the North. Frenchman met Indian here, and Englishman battled American for control. Fur was the great prize, the beaver pelts that drew men one thousand miles through the wilderness and opened up the Northwest. These woodsmen, the *coureurs de bois,* were far too busy with things like staying alive to notice what a beautiful place Mackinac was. Besides, they were not taught to look at nature that way. It was only hundreds of years later, when the last beaver had been trapped and the guns had fallen silent, that this realization came to pass. Only then did Mackinac, the focus of commerce and the prize of empires, become the "Bermuda of the North," the resort that survives today as one of the loveliest and most beguiling on the continent.

All the ancient water trade routes converged upon the Straits. The French established a settlement as early as 1670 at

13

St. Ignace. It was later abandoned but the French returned in 1715 to the shore of the Lower Peninsula to found Fort Michilimackinac. The area has been continually occupied ever since. The Indians living at the Straits had been pushed there by two aggressive and expansionist powers to the east and west. The Iroquois had wiped out all opposition on the eastern shore of Lake Huron and a remnant of the once great Huron Nation fled into Michigan. The same process was going on to the west, where the Sioux had displaced several smaller tribes from Minnesota. These uprooted tribes worked closely with the French in the fur trade and the abundance of wildlife in the new area made the living easy.

The entire area remained a French preserve for several years. Then the colonial officials in Montreal made a severe miscalculation. In 1659–60, the explorers Grosseilliers and Radisson returned from an expedition to the Lake Superior country, their canoes loaded with furs. They told of rich new lands to the northwest where the trapping exceeded anything known before. But the government of New France, instead of rewarding the men, levied a confiscatory fine on a trumped-up charge of trapping without the proper licenses. The enraged Frenchmen took their information to the court of King Charles II of England. There they received royal patronage and a company was formed to develop these rich new lands. The Hudson's Bay Company still survives, one of the oldest continuously operating firms in the world.

When the English entered the fur trade they gave the French a serious rival. They could outbid the French on pelts and their trade goods were of a higher quality. The fort at Michilimackinac became the center of this lively commerce, a focus of the tension building between the two colonial giants. Control of the fur trade was one of the underlying factors in the French and Indian War. When Montreal fell to the British, so did the key to the fur trade. The French stayed on as trappers but the profits now belonged to England.

The Straits was far removed from the American Revolution, although the British garrison was transferred to Mackinac Island in 1781 because of fears of an overland attack out of St. Louis. With the end of the war, though, Mackinac ended up on the American side of the border. The British fur traders were out-raged. They saw their livelihood being taken away from them by a ridiculous, thoughtless treaty. They held on to the island until 1796, then withdrew to nearby St. Joseph Island and bided their time. They became the strongest advocates in Canada for a renewal of hostilities with the United States and a chance to retake Mackinac.

The British lines of communication were much better than the American garrison's on Mackinac. When the actual declara-tion of war came in the summer of 1812, the forces on St. Joseph were ready to move. Under the command of Captain Charles Roberts, they sailed on July 16 and landed unopposed and unexpected on Mackinac the next day. The area where they disembarked is still known as British Landing. They quickly captured American trader Michael Dousman and sent scouting parties to warn civilian residents of the town that attack was imminent. They then seized the heights above the poorly re-paired and lightly defended fort. Lieutenant Porter Hanks, the American commander, never had a chance. He was sur-rounded, outmaneuvered, and outgunned before he even knew there was a war. The Americans surrendered without bloodshed and the garrison was allowed to retreat to Detroit—where it was captured again the following month in the fall of that outpost to the British.

The island was regarded as so important to British interests that a special relief force was sent to hold it after the fleet on the southern Lakes had been wiped out in the Battle of Lake Erie. An American attack force landed on the island in August, 1814, and promptly blundered into an Indian ambush. One-tenth of the invading force of 600 was killed. The Americans retreated and tried to blockade the island into submission. That didn't work, either. British supply ships ran the blockade on August 18 and persuaded Colonel Robert McDowall to try to capture the American ships. British raiders, led by Lieutenant Miller Wors-ley, surprised the American sloop *Tigress* on September 3 near

St. Joseph Island. Manning the captured vessel they then approached her sister ship, the *Scorpion*. The ruse worked and the Americans, finding two of their ships now in enemy hands, were forced to end the blockade.

The British, however, could not hold Mackinac at the treaty table. To the disbelief of the traders and the military, the island again wound up on the American side of the frontier. It was a terrible blow to the Canadian fur companies; for their purposes, the entire war had been fought for nothing.

The Americans lost no time in capitalizing on their advantage. In 1816 legislation was passed excluding British traders from the Mackinac area. John Jacob Astor had entered the trade in 1808 with his American Fur Company and even before the war began he was proving more than a match for the established Canadian firms. Given a free hand in the area by the U.S. government, Astor quickly turned the trade into a monopoly. By 1828 he controlled 95 percent of the fur trade on the Great Lakes. Six years later he sold out. An astute man, to say the least, Astor realized the fur trade was ending in this area. The furs were depleted and the center of activity was shifting far to the west. By 1842 it had virtually ceased to exist as an economic force at Mackinac.

At about the same time, though, the U.S. Indian agent on the island was gathering something of even more lasting importance. Henry Schoolcraft, trained as a geologist, had become enchanted with the area's Indian lore while on an expedition to the Northwest. He was named to the Mackinac post through political influence and set about assembling the tales and legends of the local tribes. His work came to the attention of a poet in Massachusetts and would be used as the basis of Henry Wadsworth Longfellow's *The Song of Hiawatha*. The success of the epic poem popularized the romance of the North country. Journalists from the East, led by *New York Post* editor William Cullen Bryant, visited the island and described its potential as a holiday resort to their readers. By the end of the Civil War Mackinac Island had become established as a vacation spot. And the crowds have never stopped coming.

The Mighty Mac

The union of Michigan's two peninsulas never has proceeded smoothly. The Lower Peninsula did not even want its northern partner in the first place. What it really was after was a slice of Ohio, the Toledo Strip, and the Upper Peninsula (U.P.) was awarded to the Michigan Territory as a consolation prize. Michigan felt it was a bit like contesting for a precious jewel and instead being given a bag of peanuts. As far as anyone knew the U.P. was just a big chunk of rocks and forest, with a commercial future as barren as its soil.

As it turned out, the U.P. held vast riches in mineral and timber reserves and its land was the making of several fortunes. But most of the wealth wound up back in the Lower Peninsula and when the trees and the ore were gone, the U.P. felt itself abandoned. There are still muttered threats of U.P. secession from the rest of the state and realignment either with Wisconsin or as a state on its own.

For more than a century, the gulf in outlook between the peninsulas was exacerbated by a literal breach, as well. The Straits of Mackinac divided them and the only link between Upper and Lower Michigan was by boat, a link that was severed often in violent winter weather. The need for a more permanent connection had been recognized as early as the 1880s. But not until November 1, 1957, did the Mackinac Bridge open, binding at least the physical gap in the state.

The 5-mile-long bridge is generally regarded as the third longest in the country, trailing only the Verrazano-Narrows in New York City and San Francisco's Golden Gate. But that's if you're counting only the main span, the distance between the two main towers (3,800 feet at Mackinac). If you measure the distance between anchorages, however, Mackinac checks in at 8,614 feet, eclipsing its other two competitors. And when the approaches are included as well, Mackinac unravels to its full length of 5 miles and 44 feet. The Oakland-Bay Bridge has a total length of 8 miles, but Mackinac goes the longer, uninterrupted distance over open water. So by that measure it is the country's longest bridge. By any measure, though, it is among the most beautiful in the world.

With its views of the traffic in the busy Straits far below, the shores of the two peninsulas, and Mackinac Island, the drive across the big bridge is an unforgettable sightseeing experience. A viewing area on the U.P. side presents equally dramatic perspectives on the engineering marvel.

Marvel is indeed the proper word. The bridge was discussed and debated for three-quarters of a century but not many people seriously believed it would ever be built. There were recommendations for its construction as far back as 1884 and Cornelius Vanderbilt added his influential voice to the chorus during a meeting of railroad executives at Mackinac's Grand Hotel in 1888. American imagination had been fired by the recent completion of the Brooklyn Bridge, and wherever there was a suitable body of water someone was suggesting bridging it. But nothing came of this idea. In the first place, the Straits of Mackinac was a good deal wider than New York's East River. And in the second, what would be the purpose of building something like this out in the wilds of northern Michigan? A fine piece of work, no doubt, but who would there be to use it? The caribou?

The plan lay dormant until 1920 when the fledgling Michigan State Highway Commission started feeling its political muscle. The revised idea called for a series of tunnels and causeways that would cross the Straits in short bounds. It was found to be financially impractical, though, and instead regular car ferry service was started in 1923. But the seed had been planted. In 1928, another idea for a bridge was conceived, with a $30 million pricetag. The Depression intervened, though, and the Public Works Administration turned down a loan application for the project in 1935.

Still the idea wouldn't die. Feasibility studies began once more in 1940. They were abandoned during World War II but immediately afterward traffic volume studies determined that revenue bonds could be repaid by users of the facility and that the bridge would generate greater traffic in both directions. The

Mackinac Bridge Authority was created in 1950 and issued $99.8 million in bonds to finance the bridge. Ground was broken in 1954 and three years later the impossible bridge was open for business.

Tourism has become the major industry of the U.P. and the bridge has been its major stimulus. The flood of summer travelers that some observers feared would inundate the area never materialized. There's still plenty of room to wander free in the U.P., a fact that delights travelers from the Lower Peninsula and aggrieves residents of the U.P. who make their living from the tourist trade. In this respect, the bridge hasn't completely bound the breaches between the two areas.

The Mighty Mac is an unqualified popular success, though. A Labor Day walk across the span, traditionally led by the governor of Michigan, is one of the best-attended summer events in the state. It makes people sentimental, too. The man who drove the first vehicle over the bridge in 1957 was so moved that when his historic station wagon was ready for scrapping twelve years later, he asked permission to drop it from the bridge into the Straits. He was turned down by the state legislature.

The bridge is open to traffic all year, but to pedestrians on Labor Day only. Fares are $1.50 for each car, including the driver and all passengers.

Fort Michilimackinac

It was only an Indian game, one of those affairs involving much whooping about after a little ball, virtually incomprehensible to the British garrison of the fort. But it was always a good show and the men came out to watch the savages at play.

It was a beautiful June day in 1763, one of the first warm spring afternoons after the endless icebound winters at the Straits of Mackinac. The fort had just celebrated the birthday of the king and a relaxed, festive mood permeated the garrison. It had been two years since the British had taken Fort Michilimackinac from the French as a part of the colonial empire that had fallen during the just-concluded French and Indian War. The Indian tribes of the Northwest, allies of the losers for the most part, were initially sullen and somewhat hostile to their new overlords. But an occasional taste of steel was bringing them around and even though there were hardly six hundred of His Majesty's Forces in the entire Northwest, it was more than enough to control the likes of these. Or so the British thought as they settled back to watch this ballgame in June.

None of them could possibly have known what had happened all across the Northwest frontier just three weeks before. On May 10, it had gone up in flame. Striking with a degree of coordination that had been regarded as impossible, the tribes fell upon the small, isolated outposts. From Fort Presque Isle on the Pennsylvania Lake Erie shore to Fort St. Joseph, a few miles inland from Lake Michigan near what is now Niles, Michigan, the outposts had been taken and the garrisons massacred. Only Detroit had been able to hold out and the village was under desperate siege against overwhelming Indian forces led by the Ottawa chief, Pontiac.

Pontiac was one of the great leaders of recorded Indian history, a mysterious figure born somewhere along the Detroit River and a comrade-in-arms of the French during the war. He watched the coming of the British with growing resentment, sensing their change in attitude toward the tribes, knowing the newcomers wanted land and represented a terrible danger to the Indians of the Northwest. Pontiac decided to act, to expel the usurpers while the chance remained. During the winter of 1762–63, he traveled throughout the country speaking to the tribes—to Chippewa and Sac, Wyandot and Potawatomi. He must have been what later generations would call a charismatic leader. He managed to convince the tribes, some of whom would just as soon war on each other as the British, to follow his direction and wipe out the invaders. Not a word of the conspiracy was leaked to the British, and when the appointed day came they were completely unprepared for the blow. Only in Detroit, where commandant Henry Gladwin had been warned by a spy, were the Indians thwarted. But Pontiac, himself, was directing that siege and Detroit would surely fall.

Vague rumors of these events had trickled in to the far-off fort at Mackinac but they were not taken seriously. This garrison, built in 1715 at the very top of Michigan's Lower Peninsula, was the northernmost outpost on the frontier. Although it was an important link in the communications route of the West, the chance of trouble from the Indians seemed remote.

The Indian game outside the fort gathered in intensity. A ball was thrown near the gates and the garrison watched amusedly as the Indians ran in pursuit. The women of the tribe sat nearby, huddling under blankets even though the day was warm. Suddenly, the Indians dashed towards the squaws. The blankets were thrown aside and there, underneath, were hatchets. Before the soldiers could react the Indians were upon them, methodically cutting them down. Within a few minutes the entire garrison was either dead or imprisoned. French traders who lived at the fort watched in horror but were left unmolested. Only the British were the targets of the Indian wrath. A handful of British civilians managed to hide in the attics of French homes and remained there until the first wave of killing subsided. They were captured the following day but a few of them, notably Alexander Henry, survived. Henry was bartered back and forth between tribes, saw British soldiers cannibalized, spent a night hiding from raging Indians on Mackinac Island in a cave full of skulls, and was rescued repeatedly by the Chippewa chief Wawatam. His account of the massacre and its aftermath, "Alexander Henry's Travels," is the most vivid surviving account of these events.

Meanwhile, Detroit had managed to survive. Pontiac had engineered several successes, including a massacre of a relief column near Fort Niagara, but as summer dragged on and Detroit still resisted, Pontiac's allies began drifting away from the siege. Finally, two schooners reached Detroit with food and reinforcements. The Indians retreated and Pontiac's Rebellion was broken. At a time when Europeans were still strung out and vulnerable, it had inflicted more damage than would any future Indian uprising. Within a few years, Pontiac had become an object of derision among his former followers. He would complain to the British that young men had beaten him and driven him from the villages. In 1769 he was murdered by a companion in Cahokia, Illinois.

By 1764 the British had returned to Fort Michilimackinac and two years later one of the most compelling personalities on the frontier took command there. Major Robert Rogers was obsessed with the search for the Northwest Passage, the all-water route to the Pacific, and he was convinced it lay somewhere to the west where the headwaters of the Columbia River supposedly rose near those of the Mississippi. While his associate Jonathan Carver searched for this route, Rogers planned an empire ruled from Mackinac, an independent province under his control.

Rogers had been a hero in the French and Indian War, leading his green-clad rangers in expeditions through New England and Quebec. But when the colonial authorities learned of his plans for Mackinac, he was recalled and put on trial for treason. Though acquitted, he was ruined financially and ended up in a London debtor's prison, drifting finally into alcoholism. Carver's book about his search for the Northwest Passage, meanwhile, became a best-seller in Europe and a shaping force on romantic European attitudes toward the Indian.

After Rogers's term of command, the fort remained active for another fourteen years. In 1781, Patrick Sinclair moved his troops to Mackinac Island and the newly completed Fort Mackinac. The original fort was abandoned. Although acquired by the state of Michigan in 1904, restoration did not begin until 1959. Today it is an excellent evocation of this period on the American frontier. The houses, barracks, and church that stood have been restored to the best degree that historical research allows. Many of the seven buildings on the grounds contain displays and dioramas, with an especially effective recreation of the massacre of 1763.

The orientation center lies squarely under an abutment of the Mackinac Bridge, and the adjoining Mackinac Maritime Museum contains a lighthouse and three historic vessels, including the reconstructed sloop *Welcome*, originally built in 1775.

The fort and maritime museum are open May 15 to October 15, from 9:00 to 5:00; mid-June to Labor Day, from 9:00 to 8:00. There is a combined admission charge to the two attractions. A reenactment of the massacre of 1763 is presented each Memorial Day weekend in a historical pageant at the fort.

A Walk on Mackinac Island

No one is sure what the name means. No one is even sure how it should be pronounced. The oldest explanation is that Mackinac can be traced to an Ojibwa word meaning "great turtle," because that's how the island appears in profile when viewed from the east. Modern scholars, however, feel the word means "place of the great fault," referring to rock formations on the adjacent mainland, or "great road," because of its importance on the trade routes. Or then again, say the scholars, it might just mean "great turtle."

The most common pronunciation is to silence the final "c" and call it Mackinaw. The word is Indian, however, not French, and a few students of the tribal dialects argue that the proper way of saying it is to click off the final "c." Even the French did it that way, and they are fastidious about their closing consonants.

However you pronounce it, Mackinac is a delight—a Michigan Brigadoon, bringing the tranquil joys of a quieter era into the midst of a more clamorous century. There are no cars allowed on the island. Transportation is accomplished by horse, carriage, bicycle, or foot. A faster pace really would make no sense. So much of Mackinac's appeal lies in the wonder of returning to streets without motors and a world without industry, where there is always time enough for everything and the leisure to get there slowly. Had Walt Disney been born in Michigan, his magic kindgom probably would have looked a lot like Mackinac.

The island is dominated by two hilltop buildings, a fort and a hotel, but there's plenty to see between them. Although you'll also want to pedal and ride, the best way to get a feel for the place is to walk. Start from the boat docks and turn right on Huron Street. (Boats leave frequently for the island from Mackinaw City and St. Ignace during the summer season. Service is reduced before Memorial Day and after Labor Day, and icy conditions generally force it to be discontinued completely between December and April.)

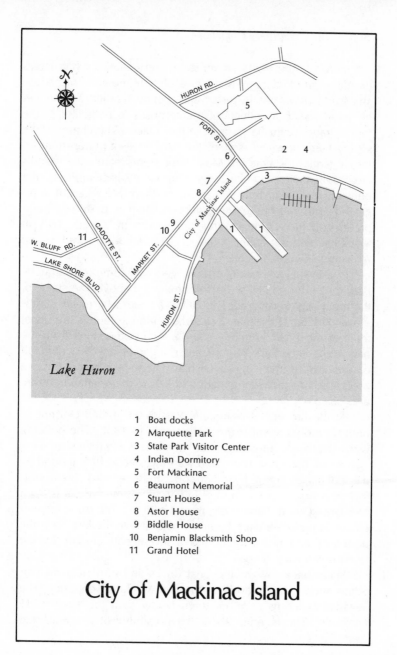

1   Boat docks
2   Marquette Park
3   State Park Visitor Center
4   Indian Dormitory
5   Fort Mackinac
6   Beaumont Memorial
7   Stuart House
8   Astor House
9   Biddle House
10 Benjamin Blacksmith Shop
11 Grand Hotel

City of Mackinac Island

Huron is the town's main street and contains what passes for glitter on Mackinac. Its ancient, white frame buildings house an assortment of hotels, restaurants, penny arcades, and souvenir stands. Such a collection of enterprises so dedicated to the tourist trade might be jarring in other places. The charm of the setting here, however, softens the hard edges and transmutes it into a gently nostalgic lilt. Most of the stores feature the island's great delicacy, chocolate fudge. The candy is ubiquitous, not only on Mackinac but throughout northern Michigan. It is regarded with much the same affection that is bestowed upon pralines in New Orleans and sachertortes in Vienna. To visit Mackinac without eating fudge is like going to Milwaukee and refusing to sample the beer.

In a few blocks along Huron, you will come to Marquette Park, once the stables of the fort on the hill above it. A statue of the great explorer-missionary, Father Jacques Marquette, stands in the park amid the lilacs. Their blooming in June is the signal for the start of the summer season. Across the street from the park is the State Park Visitor Center, a good place to acquire an orientation to the island. Displays here give an outline of Mackinac's history; combination tickets to major attractions are also on sale.

At the far end of Marquette Park is the Indian Dormitory, built by Indian agent Henry Schoolcraft in 1838. The building was used to accommodate tribe members when they visited the agency on business. The island was regarded as holy ground by the Indians and none lived here on a fulltime basis. The dormitory now houses a museum of Indian life in the area. It is open Memorial Day to Labor Day, from 11:00 to 5:00. An admission charge is included with the ticket purchase to the fort. Near the dormitory is a reconstruction of a seventeenth-century French Jesuit missionary chapel.

Walk back toward the boat docks and turn right on Fort Street, then climb the hill to the Fort Mackinac entrance. The installation looms over the town below as it has since 1781 when the British, edgy about the possibility of a Spanish-led land attack, moved the garrison to the island. Patrick Sinclair, commandant at Fort Michilimackinac, arranged the purchase of the island from the Indians for a price of 5,000 pounds. He then supervised the transfer of the garrison and engineered the fortifications, a task so well done that the structures have survived for two hundred years. For his pains he was recalled to England in 1782 on a question of expenditures and never returned to Mackinac.

The walls and south sally port, which is now the main entryway to the fort, both date from Sinclair's project. So does the Officers' Stone Quarters, the oldest surviving building in the state, with walls that vary from two and one-half to eight feet in thickness. The fort was manned until 1895 and the other eleven buildings on the ground are furnished as they would have appeared in the nineteenth century, rather than in Sinclair's time. Costumed guides conduct tours of the facility. Historic displays and dioramas are set up in several of the buildings and there are also demonstrations of cannon and musketry at intervals during the day.

Fort Mackinac is open from late May to Labor Day, from 9:00 to 6:00; the rest of September, from 10:00 to 4:00. There is an admission charge.

Return to Fort Street and descend the hill as far as Market Street. The house on the corner was once the American Fur Company store. Now it honors one of the country's great medical pioneers, Dr. William Beaumont. He was the fort surgeon here in 1822 when he received an emergency call on an accidental shooting in the store. A young French-Canadian, Alexis St. Martin, had been shot in the stomach. Beaumont repaired the gaping wound but it never fully healed. By opening a flap of skin, the doctor found he could actually observe the digestive processes occurring in St. Martin's stomach. The fascinated Beaumont began a series of experiments, taking the young man into his home and feeding him a variety of foods to see the reaction of the gastric system in each case. St. Martin was less than enthused over this bizarre existence and eventually fled.

But Beaumont had accumulated enough material for his groundbreaking work on the digestive system, published in 1833. The building, restored by the Michigan State Medical Society, contains exhibits relating to Beaumont and his work. It is open from mid-June to Labor Day, from 11:00 to 5:00. There is no admission charge.

Farther along Market Street stands the warehouse of Astor's American Fur Company, built in 1809 when the great trading monopoly was just getting organized. Joined to it is the Robert Stuart House, the home of one of Astor's top agents. The street was the center of activity during the fur trading days and the little island town was filled to overflowing in spring and summer. After the 1840s, the crowds of trappers were replaced by tourists and the two buildings became the Astor House, the island's first great resort hotel. Now the structures house a museum of the Mackinac fur trade. It is open from late May to October 1, Monday to Saturday, from 10:00 to 4:30; Sundays, 1:00 to 4:00. There is an admission charge.

The Biddle House, a few steps down the block, was also the home of a prominent trader, Edward Biddle. Dating from the 1780s, it is believed to be the oldest residence on the island. It has been restored with early nineteenth-century furnishings, as it would have appeared during the peak of the fur era. The Biddle House is open from mid-June to Labor Day, from 10:00 to 5:00; free.

Adjoining the house is the Benjamin Blacksmith Shop, an authentic nineteenth-century working forge donated by the island family who operated it for eighty years. It is open from late May to Labor Day, fom 11:00 to 5:00. There is an admission charge on a combination ticket with the fort and Indian barracks.

Turn right at Cadotte Street and begin to ascend the hill toward the second of Mackinac's great landmarks, the Grand Hotel. This rambling old resort, with its pillared, 800-foot-long front porch overlooking the Straits and sunken gardens, is one of the best-known hotels in the country. Built in 1887 as a railroad promotional enterprise, the Grand Hotel has more than survived. It has remained one of the country's preeminent resorts with outstanding recreational and lodging facilities. Although it had been modernized and touched up over the years, it still manages to retain the ambience of the century of its founding. The state of Michigan has recognized all that with a memorial plaque on the grounds, naming the hotel as a historic site, albeit a very lively one. The hotel is open from mid-May to mid-October.

From here the only reasonable way to return to town and the docks is by horse and carriage and there are always several for hire at the stand in front of the Grand.

Other Things to See

[1]   The ice can get awfully thick around the Straits of Mackinac in winter and, accordingly, the Coast Guard icebreaker *Mackinaw* is the largest such ship on the Great Lakes. The 290-foot-long vessel is powered by six, 2,000-horsepower engines and its rocking mechanism and specially designed propellers make it a formidable match for any block of ice. The *Mackinaw*'s home port is Cheboygan and free tours are offered during daylight hours when it is at berth along the Cheboygan River.

[2]   Cheboygan is also the outlet of the Inland Waterway, a 35-mile boating route connecting three inland lakes to Lake Huron. The route was known to the Indians who used it for access to the fur trading stations on Mackinac Island. The portages they had to make have been eliminated and any craft with a five-foot draft can travel the entire route to its end on Crooked Lake. The area is famed for its winter sturgeon fishing.

[3]   Bois Blanc Island guards the Lake Huron approach to the Straits. It is still largely undeveloped. Much of the land is state forest and only one settlement, Pointe Aux Pins, is on the island. Bois Blanc is accessible by daily mailboat from Cheboygan or on other rented craft.

[4]   State Highway 185 is one Michigan road that never carries a car. It is the scenic route that circles Mackinac Island and the only traffic allowed is bicycles, horses, and carriages. The circuit of the island is a lovely 8-mile trip on level ground, past rocky beaches and views across the Straits. More strenuous bike trips can be made into the interior but the shore route is an easy outing for anyone in reasonable physical condition.

[5]   Arch Rock is Mackinac's most spectacular geological formation, a stone span, fifty feet across, high above the waters of Lake Huron. It may be reached by bicycle, but an even easier way is on carriage tours from the town. The tours also ascend to the interior heights of the island for magnificent views of the lake. This part of Mackinac was once the country's second national park, created right after Yellowstone. It was returned to

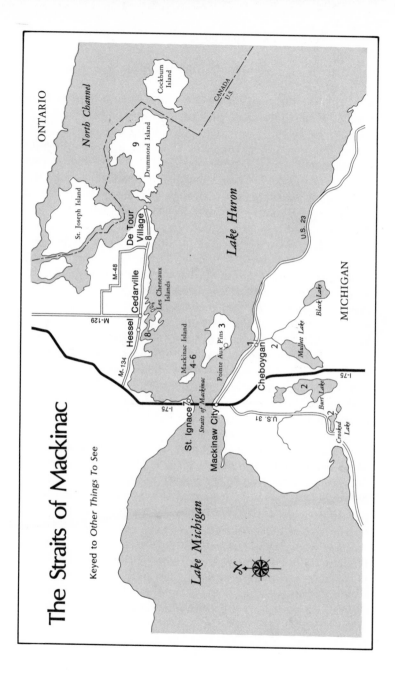

The Straits of Mackinac

Keyed to Other Things To See

the state, though, in 1895. Carriage tours run from mid-May to mid-October.

[6]   The Mission Church, at the eastern edge of the town of Mackinac, looks like a misplaced piece of New England. Built in 1830 by the Protestant Mission to the Indians at Mackinac, it is the oldest church structure in Michigan. It is now a nondenominational chapel.

[7]   Father Jacques Marquette established the mission that would grow into St. Ignace. One year after his death in 1675 on a missionary-exploring trip to the west, his body was returned here for burial from the vicinity of Ludington, Michigan. The French abandoned the mission in 1706 and the site of the grave was lost for 171 years. It is now marked by a monument on Marquette and State streets, just north of the business district on U.S. 2. Another park dedicated to the famed Jesuit adjoins Interstate 75 just off the St. Ignace approach to the Mackinac Bridge.

[8]   Michigan 134 is a lightly traveled road that runs 41 scenic miles west from Interstate 75 to De Tour. It passes through a section of Hiawatha National Forest, past spectacular viewpoints of Les Cheneaux Islands, and through roadside parks along Lake Huron. The Cheneaux ("Channel") Islands are a remote chain that offer excellent fishing and boating in a secluded setting. They may be reached by hired boat from the towns of Hessel and Cedarville.

[9]   Drummond Island was the last piece of American soil to be occupied by the British. After retreating from Mackinac (following the War of 1812), the British came to Drummond, expecting it to be on the Canadian side of the redrawn frontier. But when negotiations were concluded, Canada wound up with nearby St. Joseph Island and Drummond reverted to the United States. Thoroughly perplexed, the British left for good in 1828. Drummond is a sprawling island with several inland lakes and fine fishing for walleye and northern pike. In addition to the remains of the British fort, it also has one of the largest dolomite quarries on the Lakes. It can be reached by frequent ferry service from De Tour.

Side Trips

In Indian River, 21 miles south of Cheboygan, there is a Catholic shrine with one of the largest crucifixes in the world, a fifty-five-foot oak and bronze sculpture. Masses are held daily at the shrine, on Michigan 68 at Interstate 75.

State Parks on the Lake

Cheboygan State Park—4 miles east of Cheboygan on U.S. 23, has a broad, sandy beach on a Lake Huron bay. There are complete water-sports facilities on its 932 acres and 78 campsites.

Fort Michilimackinac State Park —no camping, but facilities for picnicking and swimming. (See page 20).

Mackinac Island State Park—no campsites, but there are picnicking facilities and hiking trails in the island interior.

Straits State Park—1 mile west of St. Ignace, on U.S. 2, has water-sports and picnicking facilities and 322 campsites.

There are two campgrounds near Lake Huron in the Hiawatha National Forest, on County Road 412 north of St. Ignace. Foley Creek, 6 miles north of the town, has 54 campsites; and Carp River, 13 miles north of town, has 44 campsites. Neither offers swimming.

De Tour State Park—10 miles west of the Drummond Island ferry dock, on Michigan 134, is a little-used, 395-acre facility. It offers swimming, picnicking, and 20 campsites.

The town of Kagawong overlooks Lake Huron's West Bay and offers one of the loveliest harbors on the Great Lakes. *Courtesy Ontario Ministry of Industry and Tourism.*

2

North Channel

Of all the roads that led to the North American West, the North Channel was the first. It went by water to the heart of the continent and was the lifeline of the vast, colonial empire of France during the 150 years of its existence.

The French had entered America along the deep highway of the St. Lawrence River, establishing settlements at the natural fortress of Quebec and the rapids at Montreal. The Iroquois tribes, hostile since their first contact with the French, blocked the way that would have led the exploring parties down the river to Lake Ontario. The explorers were turned northwest, along the Ottawa River, to search for the passage that would lead to the riches of the Orient.

They turned into the gentle Mattawa River and followed it west through a series of arduous portages to Lake Nipissing. At its far side was a westward-flowing river. Subsequent generations would call it The French. The river flowed into a great sea, which inexplicably was fresh water and not the salt of the Pacific. It was here, at the mouth of the French River, that Samuel de Champlain in 1615 became the first recorded European to see the Great Lakes.

Champlain was not struck by any great drama in the event. In his journal he writes about the squashes growing in the area and mentions his encounter with Lake Huron almost in passing. The search for the Pacific would have to go on. This wasn't it. That's what was important to him. The open waters of Georgian Bay made a forbidding crossing for the canoes of the French. They chose to remain close to shore and discovered a channel, shielded by islands from the open water, that led to the great waters beyond. This North Channel became the traditional route of the fur traders, the voyageurs who first ventured into the unknown lands to the west. Eventually they found the Mississippi, but never China.

The Channel is cut off from the rest of Georgian Bay by the great island of Manitoulin and the smaller islands Cockburn and St. Joseph. The islands actually are a continuation of the Niagara Escarpment, which arcs northwest from the Bruce Peninsula toward Michigan's Upper Peninsula. Except for a few low spots between islands, it forms a continual land bridge.

The voyageurs headed for the trading settlements around Mackinac and Sault Ste. Marie. The mainland near the Channel was a place to pass through. It was harsh, forbidding country, rocky and thinly soiled. The land is part of the Canadian Shield, the great mass of ancient rock that defines the northern limit of the Great Lakes basin. The Shield makes up almost half of Canada's land surface and here, on the northern shore of Lake Huron, it comes right to the lakefront. Once the Shield was a huge, towering mountain range, but over hundreds of millions of years it has been worn down to a rugged lowland. Forbidding as it may look, it contains riches worth more than all the pelts the voyageurs took back to Montreal.

The Shield is one of the most highly mineralized areas in the world. It has given up a million fortunes in gold, iron, nickel, copper, zinc, uranium—virtually every mineral mined. The first evidence of this wealth turned up on the shore of the North Channel at Bruce Mines. The Montreal Mining Company struck copper there in 1846. The vein gave out after thirty years, having yielded 9,653 tons of metal valued at $3.3 million.

Nickel was found near the mouth of the Whitefish River in 1848. Eight years later the first evidence of the incredible accumulation of ores in the Sudbury Basin was discovered by a surveyor whose compass ran wild in the area. Thirty years passed, however, before the full extent of this vein was realized. In the twentieth century, huge stores of uranium were found in the area north of Blind River.

Most of the big mines now lie a bit inland from the lake. The small towns between Sudbury and the Soo along the Trans-Canada Highway are relics of the lumber industry. A few of them, like Espanola, remain important pulp producers. For the most part, though, it is a lightly settled region with a small resort trade, gateway to a magnificent interior of lakes and forests.

Geographers refer to the North Channel area as the Near North. It is a transition zone, the most accessible part of the vast wilderness that stretches unbroken to the North Pole. Throughout much of it, the splash of the voyageurs' paddles still would not sound out of place.

Manitoulin Island

When the first French explorers came to the head of Georgian Bay, they discovered what they thought was a group of many islands guarding the approach to the North Channel. It was only after many years that they made a rather significant discovery. The supposed chain of islands was in reality just one enormous piece of land, so large and indented with so many bays and coves that it seemed like an entire archipelago to the confused voyageurs.

Manitoulin is the largest freshwater island yet discovered. Its 1,074 square miles cover an area larger than the state of Rhode Island. A drive of 100 miles is necessary to traverse the island from east to west and, at its widest part, it is 47 miles from north to south. That's a lot of driving for an island, but you won't mind a bit. On Manitoulin, almost every road is a scenic drive.

Take the road to Kagawong, for example. It darts out of Little Current on the northern end, climbs over ridges, then swoops down toward dark blue bays that cut deep into the land. It loops around West Bay, swings past a rushing waterfall, and finally, 30 miles after leaving Little Current, arrives in Kagawong. And after all this, what have you come to? Well, on what can pass as the main street of Kagawong there is an automobile dealership (a garage, really) that advertises "Dodge-De-Soto service." There may even be a DeSoto still lurching around town somewhere. It would hardly be surprising. That's the kind of place Kagawong and virtually all of Manitoulin is.

Although the island is quite close to some of the most populated areas of the United States and Canada, it has the feeling of being far removed—in time as well as in distance. From the south, Manitoulin is reached by a one hour and forty-five minute trip via car ferry from Tobermory, the village atop the slim finger of the Bruce Peninsula. So although it's just 195 miles from Toronto and 290 miles from Detroit, the boat ride has the effect of making the trip seem far longer. The approach from any other direction involves a long ride around the top of

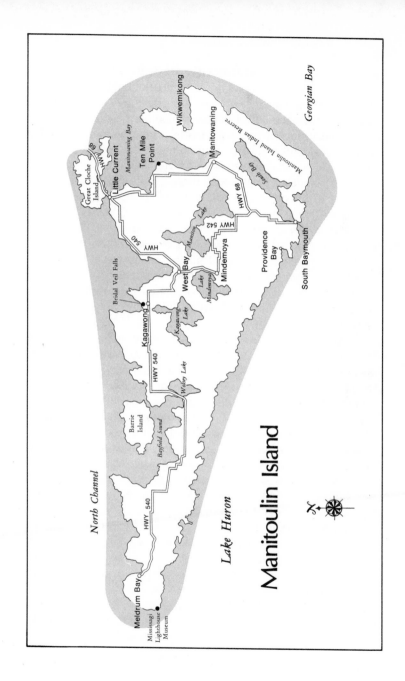

Manitoulin Island

Lake Huron, then down to Little Current across a one-lane bridge that rises for fifteen minutes every hour to permit boats to pass.

The coves and inlets which so confused the French make the island ideal for boating. Boaters come from all over the Midwest to take advantage of Manitoulin's waters. But if your cruiser has sprung a leak and all you have available is the family car, that's all right, too. There's plenty to do on land. If you stick to the coastal drives, you find yourself on spectacular overlooks high atop bluffs above the North Channel or Georgian Bay. If you head inland, you run into lovely lakes every few miles. It's easy to see why the Ojibwa felt the place was worthy of veneration. They decided it was the home of the Great Spirit, Manitou, and that is the meaning of its name.

Under the British administration of Canada, the island was set aside as an Indian preserve in 1837. The British felt some responsibility for their Indian allies in the War of 1812 and preferred to settle them in one place where they could pursue their traditional livelihoods free from white interference. They also wanted to clear the tribes out of the Bruce Peninsula and the Nottawasaga Bay area to make room for advancing white settlement. But within twenty-four years, the British decided the policy was not working. Only a handful of Indians had chosen to settle on Manitoulin, and the settlers were ready to make the leap from the mainland and bring the island under cultivation. The tribes were adamant about holding onto the island and an armed rebellion was threatened, but by 1866 the Indians were removed to the remote eastern peninsula, Wikwemikong, and the land was opened to Europeans.

For many years, the island inexplicably was a predominantly American resort, with Michigan and Ohio license plates filling the roads in summer. In recent years, however, the trend seemingly has reversed and the tourist breakdown now is about fifty-fifty from each side of the border.

The trip generally will begin with a trip aboard the M.S. *Chi-Cheemaun* ("Big Canoe"), a very comfortable, 110-vehicle capacity ferry. There are four daily summer sailings from Tobermory but reservations can be made only for the early morning and evening trips. Even then you must arrive at the dock one hour before departure time. This is not quite as onerous as it sounds. There is a comfortable, spacious waiting area at the dock and it is an easy walk from the middle of Tobermory. Reservations and schedules may be obtained from the Owen Sound Transportation Co., Owen Sound, Ontario.

The landing place is South Baymouth, a tiny, scenic settlement. An interesting stop there is the Little Red Schoolhouse, an exhibit of local history housed in what was once the town's one-room school, left just as it looked when the last class attended. It is open daily in July and August. A contribution is asked.

A far more interesting place is Manitowaning, another 18 miles north on Highway 68. This was the center of the nineteenth-century Indian settlement and a few reminders are left from those years. St. Paul's Church was built as an Indian mis-

St. Paul's Church was built as an Indian mission in 1845. *Courtesy the* Detroit Free Press.

sion in 1845 and the simple, impressive white frame building is the oldest church on the island. It's at the end of the main street, across from the lighthouse which offers a beautiful view across Manitowaning Bay. There is also a museum. This one is housed in a former jail and is dedicated to Assiginack, a local chief who was renowned as an orator. It is open daily from June to mid-October. There is an admission charge.

At the foot of the bluff below the business district is the town's most unusual sight. Berthed at a rickety old dock is the *Norisle,* the car ferry to Tobermory that preceded the *Chi-Chee-maun.* Although it was dwarfed by its successor, the *Norisle* is still a good-sized ship. In its present location it looks almost like a mirage, a battleship that has somehow wandered into a bathtub. The town hopes eventually to turn the *Norisle* into a museum.

Little Current, the largest town on the island (population 1,600), is another 21 miles north on Highway 68. At about the halfway mark, Ten Mile Point, is an unforgettable viewpoint, probably the most magnificent on the island. You gaze out over the bay, a swarm of tiny islands in the foreground, and in the distance the La Cloche Mountains. They appear snowcapped even in summer but are actually topped by bare white rock.

Little Current is a bustling place, with a pleasant waterfront business district and much activity along its coal-loading docks. It is the hub of the island's highway system. Due west is Meldrum Bay, a quiet resort town on the serene western end of the island, 83 miles away. The Mississagi Lighthouse there overlooks the strait in which Robert La Salle's ship *Griffon* is believed to have been wrecked on its homeward voyage in 1670. It is a wild, almost undeveloped area, a perfect spot for those who want to get completely away for awhile.

To the southwest of Little Current, after a twisting drive of 37 miles, is Providence Bay, with the best beach on the island. On the way you'll pass scenic Lake Mindemoya, noted for its island that resembles an old woman on her hands and knees. The lake's name means "Old Woman."

Even a short drive, like the one to Kagawong, is rewarding. Stop en route in the town of West Bay for a view of its fjordlike inlet from the waterfront park. Also look in at the Church of the Immaculate Conception, just south of Highway 540 on the turn-off to Lake Mindemoya. When the century-old church structure here burned down, the largely Ojibwa congregation decided to rebuild it in terms familiar to their own culture. So the church was constructed in the form of a council chamber, with twelve sides and rows of benches facing a central altar. It is a unique and arresting religious edifice.

Then there is Kagawong itself. Right at the outskirts of town is Bridal Veil Falls; watch closely, it's just marked as a picnic area to the right of the highway. The falls tumble into a sparkling creek which you can follow for about a mile to its outlet in the North Channel. Or, if you prefer, you can drive down a steep hill and past that DeSoto dealer to the harbor. It is one of the loveliest harbors on the Great Lakes. There are steep, wooded hills on two sides, an old church at the water's edge, a scattering of homes and stores, and a tiny park. Far out on the water, sails can be glimpsed at the mouth of the inlet. There's not much else to do besides look, but the look is well worth the drive.

Elliot Lake

The plot line is familiar from a hundred different Western movies. The lonely, persistent prospector makes the big strike. Word leaks out and a wild land rush follows, with miners flocking in from all over the country to stake out a claim. A settlement grows up in the wilderness, a boom town filled with frantic goings-on and fantastic wealth. Then without warning the vein gives out, the miners leave, the town folds up, and the wilderness reclaims the land. The scenario is as old as Tom Mix; but it all happened again, with a few twentieth-century twists, as recently as the 1950s.

Elliot Lake, about 30 miles north of the North Channel of Lake Huron, is the contemporary equivalent of Deadwood or Tombstone. But instead of a rough and ready mining camp, the Canadian government made it into a planned community that wouldn't look out of place in the suburbs of Toronto or Chicago. The metal found here wasn't gold or silver (remember, this is a twentieth-century story), but uranium. A vast deposit was discovered a few years after the atomic explosions in Hiroshima and Nagasaki. Uranium fever was at its height then and there was no stronger case than at Elliot Lake.

If you drive north on Highway 108, turning off the Trans-Canada Highway east of the old lumbering town of Blind River, you will reach this unique community in about half an hour. The major attractions are a museum of nuclear energy and tours of the area mines, but the town itself is also worth an extended look.

Elliot Lake is built in a series of concentric rings along a hillside overlooking two lakes. The various segments of the city are separated by greenbelts. You can get a quick, overall impression of the town by turning off Highway 108 at Hillside Drive South and following it around in a sweeping loop. The road eventually becomes Hillside Drive North and, just before it rejoins Highway 108, passes the Mining and Nuclear Museum. The museum, housed in the municipal building, contains some good displays on the history of the area, its underground riches, and the practical uses to which uranium is put. Like most such exhibits, the technical sections are a bit hard to grasp for those who find it impossible to hang a picture on the wall; but the information is all there for the puzzling out.

The museum is also the registration point for tours of the area mines and mills. The trips generally last about ninety minutes and it is requested that accompanying children be at least fourteen years old. The museum is open daily from July through Labor Day, 9:00 to 6:00. There is an admission charge. Mine tours are offered in July and August, Monday to Friday.

The circle tour of Elliot Lake gives scant evidence of its recent colorful past. Its story actually began in 1948, in an Ontario Department of Mines office in Sault Ste. Marie. Two prospectors fooling around with a newly acquired Geiger counter idly passed the instrument over some rock samples on a desk. To their astonishment, one batch simply labeled "Long Township" sent the counter clicking madly, indicating that it contained considerable radioactive properties. The two men combed the area north of Blind River, trying to find the test pit from which the sample had been taken. They managed to find it, eagerly tested some rocks, and found to their chagrin that the counter did nothing. There was no mistake. This was definitely the same pit from which the radioactive sample had been obtained. Still, repeated testing failed to produce a click on the counter.

Another prospector who was familiar with similar rock formations in South Africa, however, thought he knew the answer to the puzzle. He began drilling deep below the surface into the oldest rock in the area. There he found his radioactive samples, where they had lain protected from erosion that had washed away the surface vein.

Examination of geological maps showed the formation ran in a huge Z shape for 80 miles northwest of the Lake Huron shore. Presumably, the uranium vein ran along the outline of the Z. A combine headed by financier Joseph Hirshhorn knew it had to move fast to stake out this claim before word was leaked. In a series of high-security meetings they came up with a plan slightly less formidable than the Normandy invasion.

Hand-picked employees of a Hirshhorn gold mine were flown into the area under strictest secrecy and taken into the wilderness around Elliot Lake to stake claims. Accompanying them was a team of company lawyers to ensure that legal procedures were followed to the letter. Then the entire group emerged at once on July 9, 1953, to file 1,400 claims along the Z. The operation has gone down in mining lore as the Backdoor Staking Bee. Such secrecy was necessary because of the stakes involved. The United States was in the market for unlimited supplies of uranium. In those years it was the most valuable commodity imaginable and the vein was the largest yet discovered. A contract calling for the delivery of one billion dollars worth of uranium oxide by 1963 was signed, after the staking bee, by the United States and Canada.

In 1954, a road was cut through the wilds. Then it came time to build a town. The Ontario government decided it did not want a shantytown here, no rural slum defacing the wilderness. Elliot Lake, by necessity, would grow all at once; but the growth would be orderly. The government came up with the town plan that exists today, a plan that extends into the neighboring countryside of lakes and woods, to ensure an aesthetically pleasing environment.

Before the end of its first five years, however, Elliot Lake threatened to become the country's best-planned ghost town. The U.S. Atomic Energy Commission decided that a sufficient stockpile of uranium existed and cancelled all further orders. In 1960 five Elliot Lake mines closed. Production plummeted from $268.5 million to $40.5 million by 1966. Only one mine remained in operation. In a desperate move to keep the town alive, Ontario transferred an educational retraining center to Elliot Lake.

Suddenly the situation turned around. A large uranium order came in from Britain. Canada put its first nuclear power station into operation in 1967 at Kincardine, farther south on Lake Huron. Predictions about future worldwide demand for uranium were hastily revised in view of the energy crisis that began emerging in the early 1970s. Further exploration of the area was undertaken and the mines went back into operation.

Elliot Lake is a thriving, young community once more. Another mining town, Tombstone, boasted that it was "too tough to die." In the case of Elliot Lake, though, the place was just too valuable to bury.

Sudbury

A few hundred million years ago, something rather dramatic happened near Sudbury, Ontario. It may have been an enormous volcanic eruption or, as some scientists think, it could have been a meteorite slamming into the earth. Whatever it was, the results were cataclysmic. A depression measuring thirty-eight miles by seventeen miles was scooped out of the land. Large masses of molten rock were forced to the surface from deep within the earth, buckling and twisting their way into veins just below the ground. When the upheaval was concluded, the mineral-rich Sudbury Basin had been formed.

Nothing much was done about it, though, for quite a while. The Sudbury region in the late nineteenth century was still pretty much untouched and virtually unexplored. Situated upon the Canadian Shield, in a cold, inhospitable area unsuited for agriculture, there was no reason for settlement in the vicinity. Lumber companies had come in during the 1870s and quickly depleted that resource. (It was Sudbury timber that went into much of the rebuilding of Chicago after the fire of 1871.) After the trees were gone, the only thing the area seemingly had to offer was frostbite.

Thousands of miles to the west, though, British Columbia was joining the Dominion of Canada on the condition that a transcontinental railroad be built, linking it to the rest of the country. The Canadian Pacific rails reached Lake Nipissing by 1883 and began inching their way westward across the shield. The site of Sudbury was selected as an advance camp for construction crews. Blasting operations were necessary to lay track across the surrounding bare rock. It was after one of these blasts that copper deposits were first uncovered, west of town on the rim of a huge basin.

The find touched off a wild scramble, with miners replacing the recently departed railroad gangs. The first ore was shipped to a refinery with high expectations. Then the balloon popped. The refinery reported that the ore contained 2.5 percent nickel and only 4.5 percent copper, an unacceptably low amount. No one had foreseen such results. The presence of nickel was a disaster. German miners who had first identified it in copper ores said the useless stuff was the metal of the devil—Old Nick. It was difficult, if not impossible, to separate nickel from copper; and when it could be separated, the cost involved seldom justified the effort. To make it worse, the demand for nickel was very small. The Canadian deposits would only glut an already full market.

In the next few years, many developments occurred to remove these obstacles. In New Jersey, the Orford process for separating nickel economically was developed and improved. Then manufacturer Samuel Ritchie, an American who stood to lose a fortune because of his investments in the Sudbury mines, took it upon himself to find a market for all this nickel. He traveled to Britain, with the blessings of the Canadian government, and found that work was advancing there on mixing nickel with iron to make a stronger grade of steel. Ritchie saw the application this could have to armaments, for even in 1889 the European powers were preparing for a coming great war. In a famous test conducted on U.S. Navy proving grounds in Maryland, the nickel-steel plate won a convincing victory over standard steel by withstanding blasts from eight-inch guns. The news was telegraphed to every government in Europe and nickel had won its market.

Eventually, other uses were discovered for the metal and the market expanded even more. The International Nickel Company of Canada (INCO) was formed by merger in 1929 and now operates eleven mines, four mills, two smelters, a refinery, and an iron plant in the Sudbury region. The area produces 40 percent of the nickel produced in the Western world, more than half a billion pounds a year, and employs 26,000 people.

The mineral development of Sudbury has made it one of the strangest places in Canada. Its skyline is distinct—consisting of a huge smokestack and a giant five-cent piece. You can hardly miss the stack. At 1,250 feet in height it is the largest freestanding stack in the world, visible from 20 miles away on the Trans-Canada Highway. Its purpose is the dispersal of waste gas from the smelter at such a height that it drifts away over the countryside rather than descending upon Sudbury. The Big Nickel isn't quite that overwhelming; but perched atop a hill, along with other giant models of American and Canadian coins in Numismatic Park, it is an impressive sight.

Neither the big stack nor the big nickel is the most powerful image of Sudbury. It is the bare, black rock everywhere you look—not only around the INCO works, but in residential districts, around shopping centers, and along every road in town. It's exactly as if the city had been plopped down on the dead rocks and craters of the moon. Sudbury, in fact, was used as a training ground for American astronauts to prepare them for lunar landings.

The bare rock is the result of sulfide fumes from the INCO smelters. The gases, resulting from over seventy-five years of nickel production, have killed virtually all the grass in the area. The company says that new methods of growing grass eventually will green the city again. But for now it is a stark, unforgettable vision.

Sudbury is not a totally unattractive place, though. The city is built around Lake Ramsey and there is extensive waterfront parkland just a few blocks from downtown. A spacious, enclosed shopping mall is the focus of the central business district. It is also a city with a French-speaking majority, giving it a distinctive difference. There are several fine residential districts, not the least of which is Copper Cliff, in the shadow of the INCO works. This was once a totally owned company town and INCO made it as pleasant as possible for its executives— but like everyplace else in Sudbury, the patches of grass quickly give way to black rock.

Tours of the entire INCO facility, highlighted by a visit to the big stack, are given Monday through Saturday, May to Labor Day, from 9:00 to 2:30. Tours of the mining operations are not given on Saturdays. The tours leave from the north side of Copper Cliff Park, north of the Trans-Canada Highway on the west side of the stack.

Another mine tour is offered by the Falconbridge Nickel

Mines, Ltd., 12 miles east of town on Falconbridge Road. Tours begin at 9:30 and 1:30, Monday through Saturday, from mid-June to mid-September.

There is also a mine in Numismatic Park, although it is a mock-up, used to train students at a local university. A self-guiding tour enables you to examine some of the mining operations. It really is self-guiding, too. The elevator ascends as soon as it drops you off underground, and you wander around there on your own. It's a great relief when the elevator shows up again to return you to the surface. Other large coins are on display in the park, which commands impressive views over the local moonscape. The park, which also includes a model steam train and small amusement area, is open daily, May to mid-October, from 9:00 to 4:00. The hours are 8:00 A.M. to 8:00 P.M. from mid-June to Labor Day. There is an admission charge.

To get the most striking view of Sudbury, drive out Highway 144 west of town through the tailings area. Tailing is what remains in the rock after the ore has been extracted, and quite a lot of it has accumulated around Sudbury. Highway 144 runs right through the disposal area and it is one of the eeriest drives on the continent. The ride is especially impressive at dusk when slag is being poured. Locals and tourists alike head out along the road for a view of the molten metal from the smelter, a vision with which Old Nick himself would feel altogether at home.

Other Things to See

[1]   After the British moved out of St. Joseph, Major William Kingdom Rains moved in, hoping to found a colony. He had picked the place by scanning a map of Canada while on duty in Malta, and arrived at the island in 1835. There was too much cheap land available in more accessible parts of the country, though, and his scheme failed (although Rains did gain a certain amount of notoriety by fathering two sets of families with his wife and sister-in-law). A pioneer museum recounts the island's lusty pioneer history. It is located about 3 miles south of the bridge to the mainland. Open June through September, weekends and Wednesday, 2:00 to 5:00; July and August, 10:00 to 12:00 and 2:00 to 5:00 every day but Friday. A donation is asked.

[2]   The Northwest Company built a fort on St. Joseph Island in 1792 for its fur traders. Four years later, when the British gave up Mackinac Island under the long-delayed treaty provisions that ended the American Revolution, the garrison moved here. It returned to Mackinac at the outbreak of the War of 1812, leaving St. Joseph to be destroyed by American raiders in 1814. Under the next peace treaty the British not only lost Mackinac again, but also Drummond Island, which they had taken the trouble to fortify. Since St. Joseph already was in ruins, the disgruntled military abandoned the area and moved their Lake Huron base to Penetanguishene. An interpretive center at the partially restored fort recaps its frustrating history. It is located at the far end of the island from the bridge along Highway 548. Open daily, 9:00 to 6:00, from June through mid-October; free.

[3]   Ontario's copper-mining industry was born in Bruce Mines in 1846. A museum of the pioneer mining days is housed in an old church building near the center of town. The exhibits also feature a dollhouse belonging to the Marquis of Queensbury (son of the man who formulated the rules of modern boxing) who managed the mines here. The old rock dumps are a favorite haunt of collectors. The museum is open daily, late June to Labor Day, 9:00 to 9:00; free.

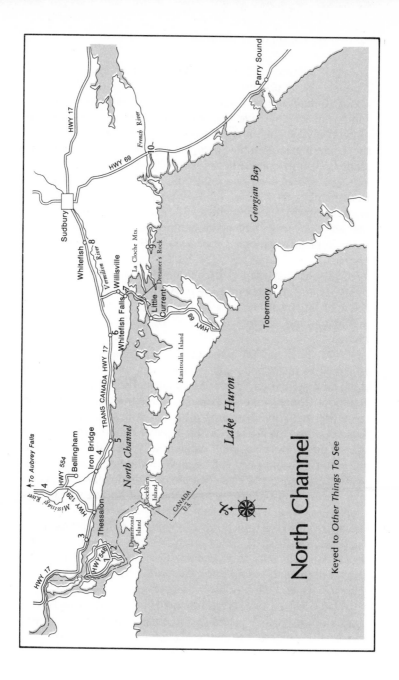

North Channel

Keyed to Other Things To See

[4]   Highway 17 heads inland west of Blind River and parallels the course of the Mississagi River for a distance of about 20 miles to Iron Bridge. From here an especially scenic, if somewhat lengthy, side trip leads up Highways 554 and 129 along the Mississagi. It is a beautiful trip through the foothills of the Laurentians. At mile 70 of the highway a short side road leads to Aubrey Falls, a noted beauty spot.

[5]   Blind River is another old lumbering town that likes to remember its history. Its Timber Village Museum, on the eastern outskirts along Highway 17, is an attempt to show what life was like in a nineteenth-century lumbering town. Open daily from July through Labor Day, 9:00 to 7:00; admission charge.

[6]   Massey started its existence as Fort La Cloche and then became a lumbering town. A museum in the middle of town on Highway 17 recalls its past. Open Monday through Saturday, June 15 to Labor Day, 10:30 to 8:30; admission charge.

[7]   Highway 68 is the northern approach to Manitoulin Island. It is an exceptionally scenic road, winding through the pink rocks of the La Cloche Mountains. The area is known as Rainbow Country after a popular series that ran on the CBC television network. The area is dotted with lakes and several lookouts over the islands of the North Channel. The highway passes directly over a small cataract at Whitefish Falls, and in town is a pleasant park with a view of the falls. The town has some picturesque old churches along its main street and occupies a very unusual setting amid the great boulders of the ancient La Cloche. Two pleasant side trips are the short, scenic drive to Willisville (just north of Whitefish Falls) and the Birch Island Lodge Road (9 miles north of Little Current). From the lodge you can walk to Dreamer's Rock, a quartzite formation that, according to Indian lore, was visited by young men of the tribe to receive holy visions.

[8]   Just east of Whitefish on Highway 17, watch for a roadside park with a waterfall and small beach on the Vermilion River—a pleasant stopping place for a rest or a picnic.

[9]   Killarney was one of the most remote villages on the Great Lakes until 1962, when a road was finally completed to the old Georgian Bay port. It's still a 67-mile haul from the main highway, and Killarney has retained much of the feel of a village content in its isolation. It is a favorite with yachtsmen and in the summer months the tiny port is filled with expensive craft. A perfect spot for really getting away from it all.

[10] The French River marks the boundary line between the districts of Parry Sound and Sudbury. On the southern side of the bridge across the historic stream on Highway 69, a plaque pays tribute to the voyageurs who passed this way 300 years ago to open up a continent. There is an adjacent picnic area.

Provincial Parks along the Lake

Killarney—adjoining the town of Killarney along Highway 637, is a sprawling 89,000-acre wilderness tract; superb canoeing and hikes through the colorful La Cloche Mountains. There are 50 campsites.

Fairbank—43 miles west-northwest of Sudbury, along Highway 658, is situated on the rim of the Sudbury Basin in a setting of birch forest. There are water-sport facilities on an inland lake and 162 campsites.

Chutes—just north of Massey, is situated on a series of waterfalls along the Aux Sables River. There is also trout fishing, swimming, and 91 campsites.

Gnarled pine trees provide a striking foreground for this view of Ontario's Georgian Bay. Courtesy Ontario Ministry of Industry and Tourism.

Huronia

Sometimes in dreams he could see the flaming image. "A cross coming from the land of the Iroquois," Father Jean de Brebeuf told his fellow priests at Ste. Marie. "Large enough to crucify us all."

In 1649, when the English colonies of America still huddled along the Atlantic seaboard, the final act of a terrible tragedy was about to be played out in a French outpost on the Georgian Bay. In its flames the first North American saints would meet their martyrdom and a mighty nation would be scattered to the winds.

Brebeuf, a mystic giant of a Jesuit, had lived in the homeland of the Huron tribe off and on since 1626. Most of the villages were concentrated on the peninsula along the eastern shore of Nottawasaga Bay. Sometimes Brebeuf had been the only European in 500 miles, absolutely alone among Indians who regarded him as a potentially dangerous sorcerer. He lived in their long huts, deciphered their language, learned their customs, and labored to bring Christianity into a hostile wilderness.

He had been sent to Huronia at the personal behest of Samuel de Champlain, governor of New France, who was anxious to win an alliance with the agricultural Hurons. The Indians were adept traders and their homeland lay just south of the access route to the fur country. The situation suited the purposes of both the Church and the empire builders in Quebec. Soon the Hurons were an integral part of the fur trade economy. A small band of Jesuit missionaries under Brebeuf became permanent residents of Huronia.

In 1639 they founded the settlement of Ste. Marie-among-the-Hurons, a central mission village to which the priests could repair in some degree of European comfort after hard months in the wilds. Even at this early date the spark that would grow into the flaming cross of Brebeuf's dreams was being lit.

The Iroquois had watched with increasing hostility the growing alliance between their traditional Huron enemies and their newly acquired enemies, the French. They decided to thwart the alliance by attacking it at its most vulnerable point—the fur trade lifeline between Huronia and Quebec.

The Iroquois began infiltrating the perimeter of the Huron homeland in 1642. Small war parties drifted up from the south. They captured twelve fur canoes and burned a village. In 1644, four fleets of canoes were sent to Quebec and only one of them made it through. This brought a detachment of twenty-two soldiers to Huronia and gave the missions a respite the following year. The soldiers were recalled after one summer, however, and the Iroquois escalated their raids.

By 1647 the Iroquois had completely severed Huronia's link with Quebec and the final stages of the war were set up. The major outlying villages were captured and torched; the noose tightened around Ste. Marie and the villages of the Huron heartland. As the tempo of Iroquois attacks quickened, conversions among the Hurons also increased. In a report to Rome dated June 2, 1648, Brebeuf counted 1,300 new baptisms. The priests were sent from Ste. Marie to satellite villages to minister to these new Christians. Father Antoine Daniel was assigned to St. Joseph, a nearby village. A large war party surrounded the place and moved in for the kill on July 4, 1648. The legends say that as the Iroquois breached the defenses, Daniel emerged from the church in full priestly vestments, drawing the wrath of the invaders upon himself and permitting many Hurons to escape.

Late in the following winter, the Iroquois returned in force, an army of more than one thousand warriors. It was a war of obliteration aimed at Ste. Marie, headquarters of the hated French. Two small villages, St. Ignace and St. Louis, lay directly in the path of attack. In the predawn darkness of March 16, 1649, the Iroquois surprised St. Ignace. The survivors retreated to St. Louis, about 6 miles from Ste. Marie. Brebeuf and Father Gabriel Lalemant were working there, and as a handful of Hurons gathered to make a stand, the two priests were urged to flee to Ste. Marie. They refused. Brebeuf had indicated in the past that he was prepared to embrace martyrdom. Now it was time. The eighty defenders of St. Louis managed to drive off two Iroquois attacks. Finally, the sheer weight of numbers broke the resistance and the invaders were upon them.

The defenders of Ste. Marie watched the smoke rising from St. Louis and knew that the village was lost. Now it was their turn to face the Iroquois. A hastily organized ambush by the still dangerous Hurons succeeded in killing more than one hundred Iroquois, including several chiefs. Discouraged, the invaders decided to withdraw on March 19 and Ste. Marie was spared. A party was sent to St. Ignace and there the tortured, mangled bodies of Brebeuf and Lalemant were found. They were returned to Ste. Marie for burial.

The mission still stood, but all around it Huronia was in ruins. Its crops were destroyed, its villages burned. The Jesuits realized that nothing could be done to withstand another Iroquois attack. On May 15, they sorrowfully put Ste. Marie to the torch and retreated to the safety of nearby Christian Island with the remaining Hurons. Half of the refugees died during the winter when crops failed in the new fields. With the spring of 1650, the new mission also was abandoned. The Hurons were moved to Quebec for resettlement and Huronia was an empty, desolate land. It would be almost two hundred years before settlers would come again.

Fathers Brebeuf, Lalemant, and Daniel were canonized by

the Roman Catholic Church in 1930 and a shrine dedicated to them and other martyrs of the era now rests on the hill above Ste. Marie. The old mission itself has been admirably restored (see following section).

The site of Ste. Marie lies just outside the bustling town of Midland. The darkly tragic lands of Huronia now echo to the cries of swimmers along broad Wasaga Beach and boaters who come to the nearby Thirty Thousand Islands for excellent sailing. Civilization has a way of catching up to even the most remote outposts.

Sainte Marie-among-the-Hurons

There is a moment of theatrical perfection here, one of the most arresting mixtures of drama and history that you are ever likely to encounter. It comes at the end of the introductory film at the orientation center of Ste. Marie-among-the-Hurons, site of the first European settlement on the Great Lakes.

The movie recapitulates the ten-year history of the Jesuit missionary village on the absolute edge of seventeenth-century civilization. At its end, the French put the village to the torch and prepare to flee from the advancing Iroquois.

"The work of ten years was gone in a matter of hours," says the voice of the narrator, "and the village of Ste. Marie was gone forever." As he speaks the words, the lights come on. The screen wall on which the movie had been shown rises and there, right behind it, is the entrance to the restored Ste. Marie, alive again after three hundred years.

It is super stuff, a charge to the imagination and the sense of history, and the village behind the walls is fully equal to its introduction. Ste. Marie really is alive, as alive as the twentieth century can make it. Artisans and Jesuits, dressed in the clothing of the time, appear as they would have looked in the original Ste. Marie. They are guides, however, and are here to show visitors what life was like and to answer their questions.

There are twenty-two buildings and a museum on the site. The air of authenticity is maintained throughout. The stables actually house animals and they smell like stables should. For one awkward moment, one is unsure whether the guide in Jesuit garb in the chapel should be addressed as "Father." In the reconstructed Huron long house, smoke from a recently banked fire billows upward into shafts of sunlight cutting through rooftop slits.

The adjoining museum helps place all this in perspective. If this museum were all that were here, the site would still be worth a visit. It is a carefully presented examination of Ste. Marie's setting in time, the reasons for its founding, and the significance of its brief life. It helps fit the events here into the larger canvas of the age in Europe and North America. The Royal Ontario Museum gets the credit for the displays.

Sainte Marie was completed in 1639, the project of Father Jerome Lalemant, who was then superior of the mission. The Jesuits had been working in the area since 1626 (see chapter introduction) and Lalemant decided they needed a central, European residence in which to regain their sense of purpose after weary months in the wilderness. He also hoped to show the Hurons what European civilization looked like. With the help of the donnes (French laymen dedicated to religious service) the settlement was built. It was burned and abandoned in 1649 after Iroquois attacks had destroyed the Huron homeland.

In time, the very location of Ste. Marie was forgotten. One hunded fifty years later, when the westward movement finally caught up to the adventurous Jesuits, surveying reports documented ancient French ruins in the area. Pioneer settlers even used some of the crumbling masonry to help build their own homes. At this point, Ste. Marie was just a legendary name from the distant past—no one knew if it had actually existed.

A few men believed, though. The Jesuit Order had been banned from Canada until 1844. When it was permitted to reenter the country, Father Pierre Chazelle headed straight for the reported ruins near Georgian Bay. He was convinced they were the remnants of Ste. Marie and the Jesuits thereafter regarded them as sacred ground. It was to be another ninety-seven years before detailed archeological excavations were carried out on the site. A small reconstruction was begun, but as the digging went on it became apparent that Ste. Marie had extended far beyond the immediate area of the crumbling stonework to encompass a wider tract than was believed possible.

Excavations were resumed on an expanded scale in 1948 and continued for four years under the direction of Dr. W. Wilfrid Jury, of the University of Western Ontario. The present reconstruction is the result of Dr. Jury's work. Teams of scholars supervised the actual building which began in 1964.

The most dramatic find on the site came in 1954. Digging within the probable lines of the Indian church of St. Joseph, researchers found a decomposed coffin. Its length, well over six feet—at a time when the average man's height was under five and a half feet—corresponded to the physical description of Father Jean de Brebeuf, who had been martyred at nearby St. Ignace during the Iroquois invasion. Further digging uncovered a lead plate bearing Brebeuf's name and the date of his birth. The gravesite is marked in the rebuilt church.

The shrine to Brebeuf and seven other priests who were martyred in Canada at the time rises on a hill across the road. The hill had been a place of pilgrimage since 1907, when it was mistakenly identified as the location of St. Ignace. A small frame chapel was built there and stood until 1925. Then, how-

The twin spires of the Martyrs Shrine can be seen above the palisades of Sainte Marie-among-the-Hurons, an impeccable reconstruction of a Jesuit mission settlement (circa 1639–49) at Midland, Ontario. *Courtesy Ontario Ministry of Industry and Tourism.*

ever, the beatification of the Canadian martyrs was announced and popular sentiment quickly grew to build a more suitable shrine. The present soaring religious edifice was opened the following year. It houses the reliquary of the martyrs, who in 1930 were elevated to sainthood.

The Martyrs Shrine occupies a lovely position on its hilltop with views over the Wye River valley and the Ste. Marie restoration. The Way of the Cross leads to the summit and a lookout over the area. The shrine is open daily, mid-May to mid-October. There is a fee charged for each car entering the grounds.

Ste. Marie-among-the-Hurons is open daily, mid-May to mid-October. The hours are 10:00 to 6:00 before Labor Day and 10:00 to 5:00 thereafter. There is an admission charge.

Penetanguishene

The rolling, five-syllable word means "place of the rolling white sands," which is in itself a mouthful. In general usage, however, the final two syllables are dropped (to the great relief of all) and the name becomes Penetang. It was the site of one of the Jesuit missions, and later its strategic location—at the head of a deep inlet at the southeastern corner of Georgian Bay—made it a likely spot for a fur-trading outpost.

Penetang's greatest days were as a naval and military base for the great British-American conflict that was expected to follow the War of 1812. This was one war that never came, however, and by the 1850s it was apparent that the place served no further purpose. The last British soldier left in 1856. The Historic Naval and Military Establishments at Penetang are a rather odd memorial to the final days of tension between the United States and Canada.

The establishment of military bases at Penetang is traceable to the sense of frustration felt by both sides following the inconclusive War of 1812. The Americans had failed in their campaign to annex Canada. The British were thwarted in their efforts to regain Mackinac and wrest control of the fur trade from John Jacob Astor's upstart American Fur Company. A sense of unfinished business hovered above the border. The Rush-Bagot Agreement of 1817 had fixed the frontier and established naval disarmament on the Great Lakes, but the British still recalled the burning of Toronto (then called York) in 1815. They were determined that the back door to Upper Canada's capital would be guarded at Georgian Bay, so the naval establishments were set up at Penetang as a defensive base, just in case.

Britain's fears were quite justified. America's hunger for new lands was a powerful force through the 1830s and 1840s. The thrust of the westward movement, though, was drawn along the inland waterways to the south and west, and Mexico's possessions became the primary target. In 1836 the annexation of Texas was accomplished by Americans infiltrating the area.

The ease with which that move was engineered, however, reawakened America's yearnings for the British territory to the north. The sentiment was fueled by widespread unemployment following the Panic of 1837. From Maine to Detroit secret lodges were organized along the border, dedicated to the invasion of Canada. Americans fervently supported William Lyon Mackenzie in his abortive insurrection at Toronto and offered him shelter on Navy Island in the Niagara River. The Canadians seized a supply ship, the *Caroline,* which was bound for him. The Americans retaliated with a seizure of their own, and for a time it seemed that war was imminent.

Meanwhile, the British army had joined the navy at Penetang. The fortress on Drummond Island had been lost under the final terms of the peace treaty and in 1828 the British withdrew. For six years Penetang was a joint base, but the growing expense of maintaining a naval base finally dictated the closing of that segment of the establishments in 1834. The army stayed on, though, preparing for the worst all through the next decade.

The war scare of the 1830s was settled by negotiation but in the 1840s it erupted again over the Oregon question. The Americans demanded all territory up to the latitude of 54° 40' and Penetang again was on alert. Once more American expansionism was deflected toward Mexico. In the outbreak of the Mexican War in 1846, any hostility toward Canada was forgotten. Afterward, America was occupied with consolidating its enormous territorial acquisitions and wrestling with the slavery problem. Tensions subsided along the border. By 1856 it was decided that Penetang could be safely demilitarized and the last British installation on the Lakes was abandoned.

Penetang today is a lovely resort community built along a ridge above its fjordlike inlet. To find the historic establishments, turn right at Robert Street at its downtown intersection with Highway 27. A left on Fox Street, then an immediate right brings you to Church Street; simply follow it out to the establishments.

Along the way you'll pass the graceful old church of St. James-on-the-Lines, built for the military in 1836. Its odd name refers to an old army term for a road. The church is situated halfway between Penetang and the establishments. When the road between the two was built, a community sprang up that came to be called The Lines. The Anglican church is noted for its extremely wide center aisle, so designed to permit soldiers to march to their pews four abreast. There are also many historic tablets and markers on the walls and in the graveyard. The church is open to visitors (except during services) from 10:00 to 6:00, mid-May to Labor day; to 5:00 until mid-October; free.

The reconstruction of the historic establishments was overseen by Dr. W. Wilfrid Jury, who was responsible for the superlative work at Ste. Marie-among-the-Hurons. Entry to the area is made in the military establishments sector. An officers' quarters has been rebuilt here and troops in period dress conduct drills on the nearby parade grounds. An orientation center explains the history and significance of the establishments.

The half-mile trip to the wharf of the naval establishments is accomplished by horse cart. A guide, drawn from history students in Canadian universities, leads a walk back to the starting point, with stops at eleven historic structures along the way. In many of them, other young guides portray the actual nineteenth-century residents of the base. Out of material drawn from diaries, letters, and historical research, the impersonators try to present a realistic picture of what life was like in this remote outpost at the edge of Empire. It is a fascinating trip, one that will hold the attention of even young children, and the enthusiastic guides do a remarkable job. Besides the huge naval storehouse and the seamen's barracks, other tour stops include the houses of the assistant surgeon, the clerk-in-charge, and the commanding officer. The tour ends in the pleasant home of the adjutant of the military establishment.

Allow two full hours for the complete tour. The establishments are open from mid-May to Labor Day, 10:00 to 6:00 daily. There is an admission charge.

Collingwood and Blue Mountain

The Niagara Escarpment cuts across the shoulder of Ontario for 250 miles, an unexpected scenic ridge above the surrounding clay and till plains. Its most famous feature is Niagara Falls, but its most scenic area may be Collingwood. Here the escarpment makes its approach to Georgian Bay, then veers to the west to run alongside the water all the way to the base of the Bruce Peninsula. Skiers, instead of water, run down the cliffside in this area. Blue Mountain, at 1,775 feet in elevation, is the highest point along the escarpment and the area just west of Collingwood has been developed as one of Ontario's leading winter resorts. The mountain has its rewards in summer, as well. The combination of blue water and adjacent hills makes it an especially pleasant stop. In addition, the broad beaches of Wasaga are just a short drive to the east.

Collingwood began life as Hurontario, still the name of its main street, a pioneer community that became an important early port on the bay. Shipbuilding was the dominant industry and the Collingwood yards remain active. One of their most recent successes is the car ferry between Tobermory and Manitoulin Island.

A museum housed in the old railroad station contains several exhibits on the town's history. It is located just east of the business district on St. Paul Street, north of Highway 26. Open mid-May to mid-October, weekends from 10:00 to 7:30; July and August, daily hours. A small admission is charged. The town also contains many fine Victorian homes on the side streets off Hurontario. One of them has been turned into a popular restaurant, the Spike and Spoon.

In recent years, the presence of the mountain has transformed Collingwood from a small manufacturing town into a full-scale resort. An energetic refugee from Hitler's Europe was the catalyst. Jozo Weider fled Czechoslovakia in 1939 and wound up here. An enthusiastic skier, he recognized the potential of Blue Mountain as a major winter facility. He also noticed something else about the mountain—its clay was perfectly

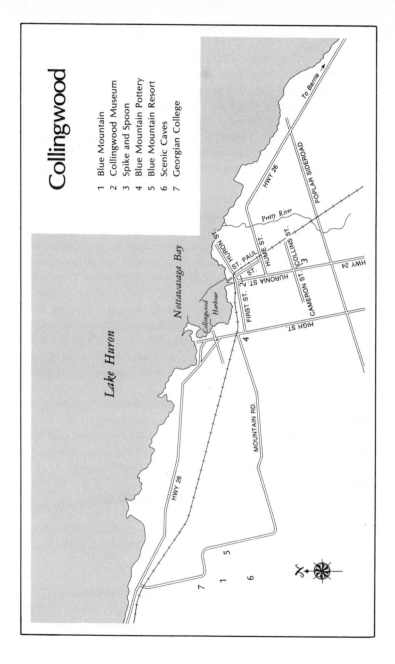

Collingwood

1 Blue Mountain
2 Collingwood Museum
3 Spike and Spoon
4 Blue Mountain Pottery
5 Blue Mountain Resort
6 Scenic Caves
7 Georgian College

Lake Huron

Nottawasaga Bay

Collingwood Harbour

Pretty River

To Barrie →

HWY 26

POPLAR SIDEROAD

HURON ST.

ST. PAUL ST.

HUME ST.

COLLINS ST.

HURONIA ST.

CAMERON ST.

FIRST ST.

HIGH ST.

HWY 24

MOUNTAIN RD.

HWY 26

suited to the making of pottery. The combination of factors caused Weider to establish two enterprises that still flourish. A short drive from downtown Collingwood (named after Admiral Nelson's second-in-command at Trafalgar) will enable you to take in both of them.

Blue Mountain Pottery is on Highway 26 and Mountain Road. It has been in operation since 1949, using clay dug from creek beds along the escarpment and fired at 2,000 degrees. The pottery offers a very pleasant guided tour through the factory with an unusually lucid explanation as to how the distinctive pieces are crafted. The tours are free and offered on week days throughout the year.

Continue west on Mountain Road and follow the signs to the south chairlift. During the winter months, six ski lifts operate in the Blue Mountain Resort; this lift is kept going in summer from July 1 to Labor Day. It is closed on Monday except on holiday weekends. There is a charge for the ride. The view from the top takes in Collingwood and its harbor and extends across the full breadth of Nottawasaga Bay. There is also a cafe at the summit.

Back at the base, the road leads to Scenic Caves, further up the hillside. However, if you'd like to see that view from the summit without paying the chairlift fee, simply continue along the gravel road about half a mile past the Scenic Caves entrance. You'll pass right by the lift and soon on your right the view from the top will be all yours for free.

Double back to Scenic Caves. It is a rather strenuous excursion, with a good deal of climbing and scrambling over rocks, and probably should not be attempted by the elderly, infirm, or very young. The attractions here are caverns and strange rock formations shaped from the limestone by subterranean upheavals along the eastern face of the escarpment. One of the rocks, the Ekarenniondi, which stands in dramatic isolation, is mentioned in Huron legend as the place all dead souls passed on their way to the afterlife. The area was inhabited by the Petuns, or the tobacco nation, who were allied with the Huron. During the Iroquois massacres of the seventeenth century, the Huron and Petun retreated into this area and used it as a natural fortress to hold off the invaders.

Ferns that do not grow anywhere else in Ontario are found in some of the deep grottoes and snow remains tucked away in corners well into summer. You can feel the temperature dropping as you descend. There is also evidence of fossilization in the rocks, indicating that the escarpment was once the floor of an inland sea.

The caves are open daily, May through October, from 8:30 to dusk; admission charge.

Georgian College, of Barrie, offers summer school programs in music and the arts on the slopes of Blue Mountain. Students and visiting artists give concerts on most evenings in late June and July at an open-air shell near the base lodge of the ski resort. For times and performers, call the school at 445-0231; concerts are free.

Other Things to See

[1]   Cruises through the Thirty Thousand Islands leave on three-hour trips throughout the summer from Parry Sound. The area supposedly contains the most intensive grouping of islands in the world. There are 10:00 and 2:00 cruises daily in July and August, with an added 6:00 cruise, Monday through Thursday. Cruises leave only at 2:00 in June, September, and the first two weeks of October. The early autumn cruises are especially spectacular.

[2]   If you would like to look at the Thirty Thousand Islands without leaving shore, follow the signs to Tower Hill from the Parry Sound business district. A lookout tower there commands a view of islands, water, and town; maybe not quite 30,000 but an eyeful nonetheless.

[3]   Honey Harbour is a resort community in the midst of Georgian Bay Islands National Park. The largest of the islands is 2,712-acre Beausoleil, with day-use and camping facilities. It is accessible by water taxi from Honey Harbour.

[4]   Port Severn is the Georgian Bay outlet of the Trenton-Severn Waterway, which begins at Trenton on Lake Ontario 240 miles to the southeast. The waterway passes through forty-five locks and Lake Simcoe on its route between the two lakes. It is regarded as one of the top boating trips in North America.

[5]   The site of St. Ignace, where Jean de Brebeuf and Gabriel Lalemant were martyred by the Iroquois, is just east of Victoria Harbour, off Highway 2. A plaque marks the spot.

[6]   Just south of the Ste. Marie-among-the-Hurons restoration, the Wye River enters a marshy area that is a showplace of the region's plant and animal life. A boardwalk, observation tower, self-guiding trails, and an underwater window help explain the lively panorama. There is also an inside display area. The Wye Marsh Wildlife Center is open from mid-May to mid-October, 10:00 to 5:00; to 6:00 until Labor Day. There is an admission charge.

[7]   Midland and Penetanguishene are starting points for cruises through the islands of the Georgian Bay National Park.

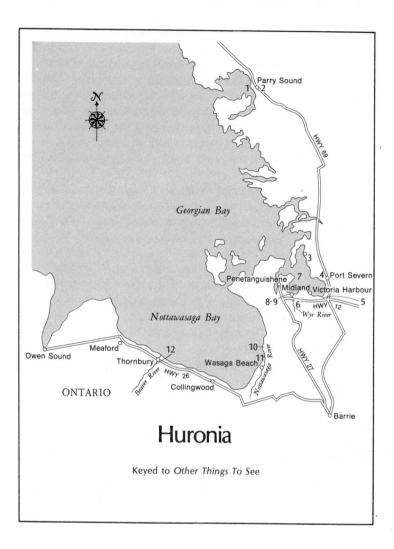

Parry Sound

1
2

HWY 69

Georgian Bay

3
Port Severn
7   4
Penetanguishene
Midland Victoria Harbour
8-9   5
6   HWY 12
Wye River

Nottawasaga Bay

10
Meaford   12
Owen Sound   Nottawasaga River
Thornbury   11
Wasaga Beach
Beaver River HWY 26
ONTARIO   Collingwood
HWY 27

Barrie

Huronia

Keyed to *Other Things To See*

The park embraces about fifty islands in this area, and others in another unit off the northern coast of the Bruce Peninsula (see chap. 4). In Midland, the cruise winds through the park for a distance of about 50 miles and lasts approximately four hours. It leaves daily at 2:00 P.M. from the Town Dock at the foot of King Street and runs from late June to Labor Day. The Penetang cruises cover much of the same area with the added attraction of a water view of the Historic Naval and Military Establishments. It leaves from the Town Dock. For scheduled departure times, call 549-7795.

[8]   Little Lake Park is Midland's leading recreational facility, built around a lake in the southwestern quadrant of town. It also houses two museums dedicated to local history. The Huron Indian Village is a reconstruction of a settlement like those that were destroyed in the Iroquois invasion of three centuries ago. It was built under the supervision of archeologists from Western Ontario University. The village is open Monday through Saturday from mid-May to mid-October, 9:00 to 6:00; 1:00 to 6:00 on Sunday; admission charge.

[9]   Also in the park is the Huronia Museum. While it, too, contains Indian displays, it is more oriented toward the pioneer setlements in the Midland area. It is open the same dates as the Indian Village, Monday through Saturday, 10:00 to 5:00; Sunday, 1:00 to 5:00; admission charge.

[10]   When the invasion of British-held Mackinac Island failed in 1814, America decided to blockade the island into submission. A British supply ship, the *Nancy,* was en route to Mackinac; the Americans set out to take her. The *Nancy* tried to hide in the Nottawasaga River, behind the sandy expanse that is now Wasaga Beach, but a shore party found her and an unrelenting bombardment sunk the lightly armed vessel in the river. Her commander, Miller Worsley, escaped, however. Within the month he led British raiding parties that captured the American ships *Tigress* and *Scorpion,* two of the vessels that had sunk the *Nancy.* The hull of the ship lay partially submerged in the river for 110 years and eventually the accumulation of silt around

her formed an island. In 1927 the hull was raised and placed on the island it had formed. Today it is the star attraction of the Museum of the Upper Lakes, which also numbers among its exhibits the complete wheelhouse of a Lakes steamer. An adjoining theater recaps the story of the *Nancy* in a sound and slide show. The museum is reached by footbridge from Mosley Street, just west of the Highway 92 bridge. It is open daily, mid-May to Labor Day, from 10:00 to 6:00; Labor Day to mid-October, until 5:00. There is an admission charge.

[11]   The eastern shore of Nottawasaga Bay is lined with some of the broadest beaches on Lake Huron and the area is composed of a virtually continuous row of summer resorts. The center of all this activity is Wasaga Beach, built on a spit of land between the bay and Nottawasaga River. It is Ontario's most intensively developed Great Lakes resort and a bit crowded in the peak season, but the beaches are flawless. A 350-acre provincial park, scattered over eight beach areas, provides excellent public access to the water.

[12]   Highway 26 between Meaford and Collingwood is the top scenic drive in the area, with the Georgian Bay on one side and the bulk of the Niagara Escarpment on the other. As an added bonus, this is apple country and in the spring the orchards along the lakefront are bursting with blossoms. The Beaver River cuts through the escarpment south of the town of Thornbury, and Eugenia Falls, where it tumbles down the hillside, is a pleasant place for a stop.

Side Trips

One of Ontario's great inland lakes resort regions lies just to the east of Huronia. From Lake Simcoe north through the Muskoka Lakes, the area is dotted with lakes and resort towns. Two of the most interesting are Orillia and Gravenhurst.

Orillia, 29 miles southeast of Highway 69 at Waubashene, occupies a narrow isthmus between Lakes Simcoe and Couchiching. There are swimming facilities on both lakes. In Couchiching Beach Park is a monument to Samuel de Champlain, first European to explore the region. It is regarded as one of the finest bronze sculptures in Canada. Also on Lake Couchiching is the home of Canada's best-known humorist, Stephen Leacock. The nineteen-room lakeside mansion has been left as a memorial to him. It is open daily, late June to Labor Day, 10:00 to 8:00; admission charge.

Gravenhurst, 45 miles east of Highway 69 via Highways 660 and 169, sits at the southern end of Lake Muskoka. Four-hour cruises across the lake to Port Carling and back are operated during the summer months aboard the *Lady Muskoka*. The cruises show off some of the Victorian showplaces built by the wealthy at the turn of the century. Two daily cruises leave from the Muskoka Wharf in July and August at 9:30 and 1:45.

Provincial Parks along the Lake

Craigleith—12 miles west of Collingwood on Highway 26, is a scenic 126-acre facility at the base of Blue Mountain. Swimming is offered but the rocky shoreline makes it inadvisable. There are 170 campsites.

Wasaga Beach—in Wasaga, offers full day-use facilities. No camping.

Georgian Bay Islands National Park—permits overnight camping on Beausoleil Island (see number 3 under Other Things to See). There are 265 campsites.

Six Mile Lake—11 miles north of Port Severn on Highway 69, covers 183 acres on an inland lake. There are boating and swimming facilities, and 192 campsites.

Oastler Lake—seven miles south of Parry Sound on Highway 69, is another inland facility with 49 acres and full watersports facilities. There are 163 campsites.

Killbear—24 miles northwest of Parry Sound on Highway 69 and a district road, is a 3,000-acre natural environment park situated along a remote part of the Georgian Bay shoreline. There are complete water facilities and 970 campsites.

Sturgeon Bay—28 miles north of Parry Sound on Highways 69 and 529, is a small park on Georgian Bay with excellent boating and fishing. There are 90 campsites.

Grundy Lake—50 miles north of Parry Sound on Highway 69, is another natural environment park, spreading over 6,310 acres and several inland lakes. There are 521 campsites.

Flowerpot Island, off the tip of the Bruce Peninsula, was named for its unusual limestone rock formations. *Courtesy Ontario Ministry of Industry and Tourism.*

4

The Huron Tract

By the 1820s it was becoming apparent that the policy of granting land in Upper Canada was a mess. The system encouraged absentee landlords to buy large tracts of land and simply ignore them, waiting for the value to rise. In addition, two-sevenths of every township was reserved by law for the crown and clergy. Since income from their sale was earmarked for these institutions, the owners also were content to wait for a better price. The problem was that the land was not going up in value. With enormous quantities of it kept from development and cheap land readily available elsewhere, the reserves remained underpopulated and undeveloped. The governments in both London and Upper Canada's capital of York decided there had to be a better way.

At about the same time, another lingering problem was coming to a head. Many residents of Upper Canada had sustained heavy losses during the War of 1812 and the government had agreed to reimburse them for damages. Unfortunately, the government in York hadn't the money to honor damage claims and the government in London was tired of pouring its wealth into this troublesome, unprofitable province. A commission was

79

organized in England to deal with the problem and find an equitable solution. One of the men selected to serve on the commission was a Scottish novelist, John Galt. He had worked up a fine sense of outrage over the treatment of these war-impoverished Canadians and threw himself enthusiastically into the job of seeking redress for them. Eventually, he became convinced that the revenue from the sale of the unused Crown Reserves could provide the needed funds. He found backers in the Colonial Office and a willing group of London financiers to put up the capital. In 1824 the Canada Company was formed and received a 1.1 million-acre block of land in the western part of the province. It extended all the way to Lake Huron and became known as the Huron Tract.

Galt was fired with zeal. He crossed the Atlantic in 1826 and started making plans for the promotion and management of this huge chunk of territory. He brought with him a literary friend from Scotland, Dr. William "Tiger" Dunlop, who was appointed to the post of Warden of the Forests. The two of them happily set out to explore the property, laying out a town here, planning a road there, and generally having the time of their lives. The town of Guelph was designed for the eastern end of the tract, but Galt and Dunlop agreed that the future of the Canada Company lay on the Huron shore. Dunlop, accordingly, was dispatched to find a proper site for company headquarters in 1827. He settled on an area at the mouth of the Maitland River, which grew into the town of Goderich.

Dunlop is one of the most intriguing figures in Ontario's history. He had fought in the War of 1812, seeing action at the bloody engagements of Lundy's Lane and Chippawa. Afterward, he went to India with his regiment and his hunting feats there won him the lifelong nickname of "Tiger." He turned to writing upon his return to England and there struck up a friendship with Galt. Besides being a soldier, hunter, and writer, Dunlop was also a noted wit. When Goderich was still little more than a collection of cabins in a clearing, Dunlop organized a yacht club with himself as captain. A British visitor indignantly reported that at the time of his visit there "the harbor contained three craft of the smallest size and I did not see a boat or yacht of any description." Some are always slow to see the jest. During the Rebellion of 1837, Dunlop led Huron's Loyalist detachments, one of which bore the inspired and fearsome name of the "Bloody Useless." He is best remembered, though, for his will, in which he managed to get off a final witty shot at each member of his family. It is a model document for anyone who wants to leave something to be remembered by.

Galt soon ran afoul of the ultra-conservative aristocrats in York and was removed from his post with the company. The enterprise prospered, however, and Dunlop stayed on at Goderich until his death. Contrary to the reckonings of both Dunlop and Galt, the town never grew into a great port; it is, in fact, much smaller than Guelph. The Lake Huron shipping lanes lie primarily on the American side of the water and whatever prosperity came to Goderich was largely a function of the city's salt deposits. Even this was discovered in a haphazard fashion. What the developers were really looking for was oil. Fired by the discovery of petroleum reserves east of Sarnia, they drilled to the 700-foot level and then gave up. But Samuel Platt took over the operation and persisted in the drilling. He struck pure brine and soon Goderich was processing 100 barrels a day. The Sifto Mine today operates at the 1,760-foot level, extends under the floor of the lake, and produces 1.5 million tons of rock salt each year.

Owen Sound

It was not easy being a Canadian artist in the early years of this century. "It's bad enough to have to live in this country, without having pictures of it in your home," one woman told painter A. Y. Jackson. Yet shortly before World War I, a group of young men came together in Toronto and set out to paint the Canadian landscape in a manner freed of European academic traditions and restraints. It was to be a Canada viewed through Canadian eyes—with bright colors, native themes, and bold composition. They called themselves the Group of Seven. Each summer they journeyed to a remote corner of the north, then returned to Toronto over the winter to paint what they had seen. They went to Algonquin Park and the Algoma district, showing the magnificent regions to the rest of the country in their canvases, and instilling a new appreciation of Canada's landscape in its people.

Although Tom Thomson was closely associated with the others, he is not numbered in the Group of Seven. He worked with many of them as a commercial illustrator, traveled with them to the north, and shared studio space with them in Toronto; but while his companions went on to success and acclamation, Thomson died in 1917 at the age of forty. He drowned in Algonquin Park while canoeing alone, on a calm day, on a lake he had painted many times. Over the years he has become the most romantic figure in Canadian art, a genius cut short at the height of his powers.

This Georgian Bay port town was Thomson's home for half his life. He grew up on the nearby family farm and worked in a foundry in town before leaving for good at the age of twenty-one. Owen Sound now operates the Tom Thomson Memorial Gallery and Museum, housed in a striking structure on the Sydenham River near the city's center. It displays personal memorabilia of Thomson along with paintings by him and his contemporaries.

Owen Sound is a good place for a landscape artist to grow up. The city occupies a valley carved from the Niagara Escarpment by the Sydenham on its way to Georgian Bay. The original tribal name for the place was Wadineednon, or Beautiful Valley, a fair enough description. The Europeans who settled the town in 1840 sought to improve on the Indian name by first calling it Sydenham, then changing its name to that of the adjoining deep inlet of Georgian Bay. That body of water was named for Captain William Fitzwilliam Owen, who produced the first complete charts of this portion of Lake Huron in 1815.

It is a splendidly scenic place with its surrounding green hills and views across the water. Harrison Park, on the town's southern edge, is exceptionally attractive—a 125-acre municipal facility on the river with waterfalls, campgrounds, nature trails, waterfowl areas, and gardens. There are portions of it that seem miles away from any city. Thomson must have roamed the area as a boy and it prepared his eye for what would follow.

Twelve years after leaving Owen Sound he joined the firm of Grip Limited in Toronto. There he met the head designer, J. E. H. MacDonald, and a group of four younger men who worked for the company: Arthur Lismer, Fred Varley, Frank Carmichael, and Frank Johnston. These Grip employes formed the nucleus of the Group of Seven. They were later joined by a wealthy patron-artist Lawren Harris and Montreal-born A. Y. Jackson. Amid the intellectual ferment in the Grip offices, Thomson's ideas about art began to take form. He made his first trip to Algonquin Park in 1912, sketching landscapes of lakes and woods with meticulous care. In 1913 his canvas *A Northern Lake* was entered in a competition and purchased by the government of Ontario. It now hangs in the Ontario prime minister's office.

Through the financial aid of friends, Thomson was able to quit his job and paint full time in 1914. He shared space in the group's studio (financed by Harris), later moving into a shack behind the building. He spent the next three summers in Algonquin, attracting a growing following of Canadians who recognized in him the fountainhead of an important new movement. He was able to capture the awesome silence and somber majesty of the north better than any other man, and even in his lifetime this was appreciated. Then in 1917 he drowned. How an expert canoeist in an area with which he was intimately familiar could have lost his life in such a manner has never been adequately explained. It is the stuff of legend.

The permanent collection of the Thomson Gallery in Owen Sound will give you some idea of his work. More of his best pieces are on exhibit at the National Gallery of Canada, Ottawa, while the great showcase of the Group of Seven is the McMichael Collection in Kleinburg, outside of Toronto. The gallery is open daily except Monday, noon to 5:00; on Wednesday and Friday, from 7:00 P.M. to 9:00 P.M. In July and August it is open every day. There is an admission charge.

There is a second excellent museum in Owen Sound which, like the Thomson Gallery, was a 1967 centennial project. The County of Grey-Owen Sound Museum traces the history of the area from geologic times to the pioneer era. Notable displays include a scale model Ojibwa village, a twenty-six-foot-long birchbark canoe (made in 1973), and demonstrations of pioneer crafts. The central exhibits are housed in a modern structure. Also on the grounds are two log houses, furnished in the manner of 1840 and 1900, and a blacksmith shop. The museum is open Monday, Wednesday, Friday, and Saturday in July and August, 9:00 to 5:00; on Tuesday and Thursday, to 8:00; and on Sunday, 1:00 to 5:00. In other months, the hours are 1:00 to 5:00, with a Monday closing. The entire museum closes from December 15 to January 15 and the outlying buildings close through March. There is an admission charge. The museum is located on Highway 6 and Sixth Street East.

The Bruce Peninsula

The Bruce has appeared differently to the various men who have seen it. To Samuel de Champlain, who caught a glimpse of the peninsula during his voyage of exploration in 1615, it was reminiscent of the rocky shores of his native Brittany. To the Scottish settlers of the nineteenth century, it called to mind the headlands of the home island. When they began moving into the area it was still known by its Indian name, Saugeen. The Scots changed it to Bruce in a nostalgic gesture toward home.

To the explorers of the long years between these centuries, it was an ominous, unknown, unnamed land. It was not even clearly charted until 1815, 200 years after Champlain, because its forbidding cliffs and treacherous coastline kept even the heartiest sailor at bay. Into the present century it was a place of dread for mariners, and the list of vessels lost off its shore is a long and deadly one.

To the land-based traveler, however, the Bruce is a place of inspiring beauty. Even its melancholy record of shipwrecks is partially preserved in a unique underwater park off the northern coast. The land tilts to the west, with the Niagara Escarpment running along its eastern shore. So on its Georgian Bay side the Bruce is a place of huge rock walls and rugged capes, but at the base of its western edge are the broad, gentle beaches of Lake Huron. The two sides of the peninsula look as if they belong to two different pieces of land.

The Bruce is one of the most prominent geographic features of the Great Lakes. It cuts Lake Huron almost in half and does, in effect, seal off the Georgian Bay. Early explorers listed the bay as a sixth and separate lake, and in many respects it is an entirely Canadian Great Lake.

The Bruce was purchased from the Ojibwa in 1854, the last significant land acquisition in southern Ontario. Soon the first wave of settlers washed over the area. Many of them quickly washed right back out again. An odd land-use law withheld all timber rights from the new settlers and required that special requests be filed even for clearing the land. The soil was no great bargain to begin with and this added impediment was more than enough to discourage the first farmers. Lumber companies then moved in and emptied the peninsula of its trees. The law eventually was rewritten, but by then there were very few timber rights to worry about.

It is a 99-mile drive along Highway 6 from the base of the Bruce to its head at Tobermory. Except for a few miles around Wiarton, you can drive the entire route and never have the slightest inkling that you're near the water. You must get on the side roads to find the real Bruce. There are no outstanding scenic drives, but poke around at your own pace and you'll find some vistas to remember.

For the best swimming, the favored stop is Sauble Beach at the southwestern corner of the peninsula. There is a wide and sandy public beach there, and just north of it is a provincial park with a waterfall and good trout fishing. For even better fishing, Oliphant is the supply point for the aptly named Fishing Islands. Named for the commercial fisheries that flourished here a century ago, the islands no longer sustain fishing on such a large scale, but they still are noted for their yield of bass, perch, and pike.

Across the peninsula is Wiarton, the metropolis of the Bruce with a population of 2,100. There is a fish hatchery just north of town along Colpoy Bay that welcomes visitors. It is situated adjacent to Spirit Rock, an attractive lookout point. If you are not pressed for time, you can continue along the bay and follow the signs to the Cape Croker Indian Reserve. Here you can view the fine cliffside scenery, a picturesque lighthouse at the top of the cape, and some Indian craft shops. The reserve is about 15 miles from Wiarton on county roads.

A more accessible beauty spot is the village of Lions Head. Situated at the base of Isthmus Bay, the place is named for a rock formation on one of the towering cliffs that guard the entrance to the little bay. There is a pleasant beachfront park in town, and another picnic area on the scenic bay drive that runs north of Lions Head. It is a magnificent location and Isthmus Bay is a name that really does not do it justice. The place is probably the most photogenic on the peninsula and well worth the short detour from Highway 6.

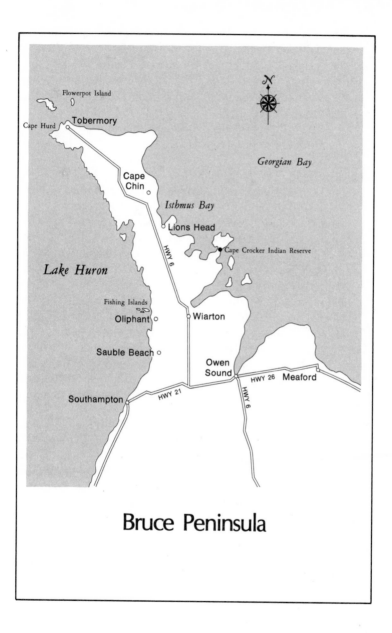

Bruce Peninsula

There is a road that runs from Lions Head to Cape Chin, but it is a challenge to find it (and once having been located, to remain on it). It is far easier to return to Highway 6 and then take the turnoff marked Cape Chin. Here is another beauty spot of the Bruce—St. Margaret's, a charming replica of a British country stone church that was opened in 1928.

Just south of Tobermory is the best museum on the Bruce. The Peninsula and St. Edmunds Township Museum, housed in an old school building, displays items relating to the history of the area. It is open daily from July 1 to Labor Day, 10:00 to 9:00; open weekends other months, from mid-May to mid-October, 1:00 to 5:00. There is an admission charge.

Finally, at land's end, is Tobermory. Its two harbors, Big Tub and Little Tub, are conveniently divided by a natural limestone wall. Big Tub is the departure point for the ferry to Manitoulin Island (see chap. 2). Little Tub is the site of a marina and is surrounded by shops and eating places.

Although this is land's end, it is certainly not the limit to sightseeing on the Bruce. The Flowerpot Island unit of Georgian Bay Islands National Park is just offshore, accessible by boat taxi service from Little Tub. The island's unique rock formations (and name) result from the greater solubility of the limestone base rock, leaving the dolomite cap rock to hang over the base like a vase of blooming flowers. There are trails and camping facilities on the island, as well as a picnic area.

For the more adventuresome, Fathom Five Provincial Park provides the most fascinating diving experience on the Great Lakes. The park encompasses about fifty square miles of the Cape Hurd archipelago and beneath its waters lie fifty known shipwrecks, a unique museum of antique shipping preserved like mummified pharoahs. Visitors can rent boats and equipment at Little Tub and should register at the park headquarters. The park is still under development and eventually there are plans for an underwater viewing facility for the less athletic. For those with scuba experience, though, it is a treasure house. The visitor center at Little Tub is open from May through September.

Goderich

If you were to sit down and try to imagine the sort of small town you wished you had grown up in, it would probably come out looking very much like Goderich—a shady courthouse square, tree-lined streets fronted by immaculate cream brick homes, church spires rising through the branches, a beach, a museum to poke around, Sunday band concerts in the park, a lighthouse, bits and pieces of history scattered about, a picturesque country inn just a few miles away. All of these scenes are the stuff of memory and a few faded photographs in an old scrapbook. But it still thrives in this Lake Huron port and, because this is Canada, there is even a green for lawn bowling.

Goderich is the sort of place you expect might have resulted from the town planning efforts of a pair of Scottish literary gentlemen. Novelist John Galt and his friend Dr. William "Tiger" Dunlop drew up the circle-in-a-square design for the center of town. It is not especially practical for traffic flow and other mundane considerations, but it certainly is pretty. Although the hub of this design is called The Square, it is actually an octagon. The courthouse occupies a tree-filled tract in its center. Four streets named for the primary directions flow into the center, along with four others that angle toward the compass points in between. The whole arrangement is bounded on a two-block radius by four main thoroughfares, creating the squared circle. It sounds confusing (and it is), but it is ideal for strolling; and at each point where one of the angled streets intersects the main artery, there is a flowering park. Galt and Dunlop knew what they were doing.

Take a walk around the square and its surrounding business establishments. At various times of the year there are exhibits in the courthouse park, and on the fourth weekend of July, a Festival of the Arts is held there. From this point, the most interesting streets for walking are North Street, Colborne Street, West Street, and Montreal Street.

Try North Street first. Two blocks up, past a group of churches, is one of Goderich's major sights—the Huron County

Pioneer Museum. Almost every county town in Ontario has an institution like this. The museums are, for the most part, praiseworthy efforts by history-minded residents, based on the idea that the everyday life of their forebears is worthy of display and memorialization. Most of them, however, are well-meaning duds. Poor organization, incoherent labeling, and exhibits that make sense only to other locals defeat their intent. Goderich is the exception. Its historical museum can stand with any around the Great Lakes. The displays are attractive and imaginatively presented, and they follow through on identifiable themes. Typical nineteenth-century shops are outfitted as they would have appeared, from a smithy's to a dentist's office. Displays on activities like flour-milling and sawing lumber show how the pioneers performed their routine labors. The development of farm machinery is emphasized with a hall of antique harvesters, threshers, and other agricultural vehicles. The displays fill twenty rooms in six structures. The museum is open daily from May through October; Monday through Saturday from 9:00 to 5:30, Sunday 1:00 to 5:30. The museum is also open every day but Sunday in April.

The town's other big historical attraction is a few more blocks to the northeast. Continue along North Street to Gloucester Terrace, then turn right to Victoria Street. At the intersection is the Huron Historic Gaol, dating from 1842—the oldest public building in western Ontario. The design of the courthouse area must have been utterly fascinating for Goderich's founders, because when it came time to build this penal structure, it also was built in the shape of an octagon. Since Dr. Dunlop had a hand in the planning, it is easy to guess where the idea originated.

The gaol served its intended function until 1972 and so remains almost perfectly preserved. Its two-foot-thick walls, bare cells, and endlessly spiraling staircase present a pretty grim picture. Actually, the structure was regarded as a model of nineteenth-century penology, humanely planned by liberal men who rejected the idea that suffering should play a part in incarceration. There were several individual exercise yards, and the separate blocks enabled the warden to classify prisoners, keeping the hardened criminals away from the petty offenders.

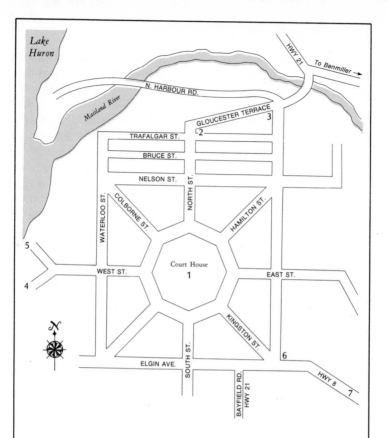

1 Court House
2 Huron County Pioneer Museum
3 Huron County Jail
4 Lighthouse Park
5 Harbour Park
6 Tourist and Development Office
7 The Pillars

Goderich

In the tower room, originally intended as a chapel, was Dr. Dunlop's court. It now contains memorabilia of that singular fellow, including a copy of his famous will. An excellent self-guiding tour of the building and its precincts may be taken with the help of a pamphlet issued upon entrance. Included in the tour is a visit to the restored quarters of the gaol's governor, built in 1900. The gaol is open from June to mid-September, Monday through Saturday, 10:00 to 6:00; Sunday, 12:00 to 6:00. A donation is requested.

Return to the courthouse square and this time head out West Street. This handsome avenue of striking old homes leads to the beach and several parks. At the fork of the road, turn left to see Lighthouse Park, a bluff-top facility with fine views of the lake and harbor. It is adorned with historic anchors and chains from lake vessels. The *National Geographic Magazine* once proclaimed the sunsets on this stretch of Lake Huron to be among the most colorful in the world. Each lake town, of course, claims that theirs are the best of all, but the sunsets from Lighthouse Park are pretty hard to top.

Back at the road fork, a right turn will lead you to Harbour Park. This is the site of Dunlop's first cabin and its band shell houses the Sunday night summer concerts. The road continues down the bluff to the town beach. It is a wide, sandy expanse, but its charms are mitigated somewhat by the adjacent port installation at the mouth of the Maitland River.

There are a few other points of interest around Goderich. Just across the Maitland on Highway 21 is the tomb of Dr. Dunlop. It takes a bit of a climb to reach its perch on a ridge above the river, but it is a fine lookout spot and a fitting memorial to the man. If you head east from town on Highway 9 toward Clinton, you will pass The Pillars, a handsome stone memorial to the pioneers who opened up the Huron Tract and came here on the long road from Guelph.

Continue along Highway 9 to Huron County Road 1 and you will come upon signs directing travelers to the Benmiller Inn. This is a unique country hotel, built with a historic sense that compares to the paradors of Spain. The two hotel structures are built around a pair of nineteenth-century mills on the Maitland. As much original material as possible was incorporated in the hotel's design and the furnishings of its rooms, and other pieces from the same era were rescued from demolished buildings in Toronto and London. It also commands a lovely riverside location adjacent to a natural reserve. The inn generally is jammed on summer weekends and advance reservations are essential. It makes a pleasant stop, however, for lunch or dinner.

Other Things to See

[1] A place with an outstanding public beach is South-ampton, outlet of the Saugeen River to Lake Huron. The Bruce County Museum here is housed in an 1878 schoolhouse and contains historical exhibits on the area. It is located on Victoria Street at High Street, one block east of Highway 21. It is open July and August, Monday through Saturday, 10:30 to 5:00; Sunday, 1:30 to 5:00. In May, June, September, and October it is open daily, 2:00 to 5:00. There is an admission charge.

[2] Port Elgin, another of the Scotch lakeshore towns, is a place well endowed with maples. Follow Green Street from Highway 21 to the beach to see the trees at their shadiest. There is a fine public beach in town and a children's miniature railroad. The tracks run along the water in North Shore Park, and the train operates daily from mid-May to mid-October; there is a charge for the ride.

[3] Canada's first nuclear power center is located just north of Kincardine, near the town of Tiverton. Watch for the signs marked "Visitor Centre" on Highway 21. The Bruce Nuclear Power Development is open for tours in July and August, Wednesday through Sunday, from 10:30 to 5:00; free. The Visitor Centre is open daily during the same hours.

[4] Many of Kincardine's settlers came from the Scottish Hebrides and when the town was incorporated in 1875, it was named after the earl of Elgin and Kincardine, whose lands included those islands. The town still clings to its Scottish heritage and every Saturday night in July and August there is a pipe band parade and concert. The town's swimming area is named Boiler Beach after the spectacular explosion of the *Erie Belle* in 1883 just offshore.

[5] There are several historic and photogenic lighthouses along this section of Lake Huron in Bruce County. An Ontario historic plaque marks the Point Clark Light near Amberley. The one at Kincardine overlooks the town's harbor and is painted an especially vivid red and white. Southampton's lighthouse is so popular with photographers that it is used as a commercial symbol for the town.

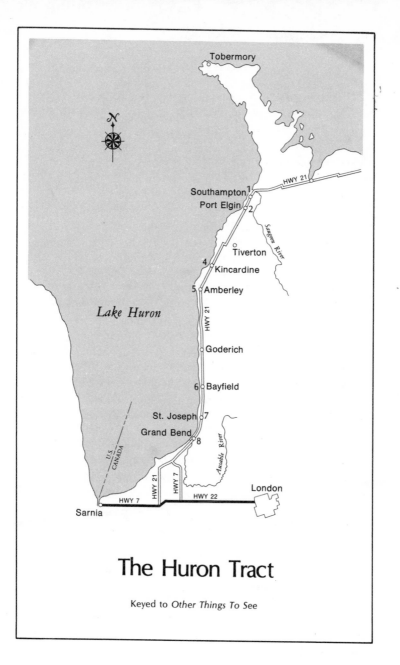

Tobermory

HWY 21

Southampton 1
Port Elgin 2

Saugeen River

Tiverton

4 Kincardine

5 Amberley

Lake Huron

HWY 21

Goderich

6 Bayfield

St. Joseph 7

Grand Bend 8

Ausable River

London

U.S. CANADA

HWY 21   HWY 7

HWY 7   HWY 22

Sarnia

The Huron Tract

Keyed to *Other Things To See*

[6]   Surveyor Henry Wolsey Bayfield named many of the geographical features of the Lake Huron shore after British military heroes and officials of George III's government, but one of the prettiest of the lakeshore villages was named after him. Bayfield is a charming little place with a large, tree-shaded green and striking old homes. The Little Inn started life as a stagecoach stop in 1848 and still dispenses rooms and cheer to travelers. There is an adjacent marina on the Bayfield River. The village is one of Ontario's best-kept secrets.

[7]   If Narcisse Cantin's dream had been realized, St. Joseph would have been a booming metropolis today while the cities of Detroit and Toledo would have turned into comparative backwaters. Cantin was an early promoter of the Great Lakes Seaway system, but his plan also called for a trans-Ontario canal, from Port Stanley on Lake Erie to St. Joseph on Lake Huron. It would have saved several hundred miles in distance and kept all that commerce in Canada, too. Fortunately for Detroit and Toledo, Cantin's vigorous drumbeating came to naught. St. Joseph has dwindled into a simple crossroads, marked only by a plaque for Cantin's nice try.

[8]   Grand Bend is the busiest of the Lake Huron beach resorts, a bustling little town on the Ausable River that fills to the brim during the summer. Main Street, in the few blocks between Highway 21 and the beach, is jammed with shops devoted to the seasonal trade. Amid the hubbub there is also a pioneer museum located on the site of the village's first Presbyterian church. The Eisenbach Museum is open daily from mid-May to mid-October; there is an admission charge.

Side Trips

London, 40 miles southeast of Grand Bend, is Canada's ninth largest city. Situated on the River Thames, just like its larger namesake, it is the seat of the University of Western Ontario's lovely campus. Its Storybook Gardens in Springbank Park is one of the country's top children's attractions, with fairy-tale characters recreated in a garden setting. The gardens are open mid-April to mid-October. There is an admission charge. Fanshawe Pioneer Village, northeast of town, is a reconstructed pioneer settlement. It is open daily, 10:00 to 5:00, mid-May through September; admission fee.

Stratford, 45 miles southeast of Goderich, is the site of one of the continent's top dramatic festivals. While focusing on the works of William Shakespeare, the Stratford Festival also includes contemporary drama, classical theater, folk performances, and opera. The festival, which began modestly in 1953, is now regarded as a top theatrical event and during the summer months the little town on the Avon River becomes one of the tourist centers of North America. Its season runs from late May to late October; check locally for times and schedules of performances. For nontheatergoers, there are 130 acres of parks and gardens lining the Avon in town.

Provincial Parks along the Lake

Ipperwash—12 miles southwest of Grand Bend, is a 201-acre park on the lake with an excellent sandy beach and a full range of water-sports facilities. There are 264 campsites.

Pinery—5 miles southwest of Grand Bend, is a sprawling 5,350-acre tract. It encompasses rolling sand dunes, a 6,000-foot beach, nature trails, canoeing on the Ausable River, and a full assortment of sports facilities for both the summer and winter seasons. There are 1,000 campsites.

Point Farms—4 miles north of Goderich, occupies a 582-acre lakefront area and is built around a restored barn. The old building is the site of several activities, including barn dancing. There are also water-sports facilities, a beach, and 200 campsites.

Inverhuron—13 miles north of Kincardine, is a day-use beach facility within sight of the Bruce Nuclear Power Plant.

Sauble Falls—2 miles north of Sauble Beach, lies along a waterfall on the Sauble River. There is swimming at nearby beach areas, but no beach within the park. There are 154 campsites.

Cyprus Lake—8 miles south of Tobermory, is a natural environment park that is situated on both an inland lake and Georgian Bay. It offers water-sports facilities and spectacular hiking trails along the Niagara Escarpment above the bay. There are 244 campsites.

Fanciful statues of animals and nymphs grace the fountains at Cranbrook. *Courtesy the Detroit Free Press.*

5

...and Sometimes St. Clair

St. Clair is a lake with an identity problem. It's a good-sized body of water at 460 square miles and if it were located almost anyplace else in the United States or Canada it would dominate the area's geography. But situated as it is, right in the middle of the Great Lakes system, it is almost unnoticed, dwarfed by its gigantic neighbors. Listings of the Lakes include St. Clair almost as an afterthought, much like the letter "y" is tacked on at the end of the list of vowels.

Even the origins of its name are somewhat muddled. According to the traditional account, Robert La Salle's ship, the *Griffon*, entered the lake on St. Claire's Day, August 12, 1679, and it was named accordingly by the explorer. A different explanation evolved along the St. Clair River, which connects the lake to Lake Huron. This story was that the name originated with Patrick Sinclair, a British military man who is best known as the builder of Fort Mackinac. He erected a stockade in the area around 1764 and eventually gave his own name to the community. Later it was changed to Palmer, but the belief developed that the original name had become attached to the adjacent river and lake and over the years had been corrupted from Sinclair to St. Clair. A few early historians even believed that name was derived from Arthur St. Clair, first governor of the old Northwest Territory. Most contemporary scholars credit the name to the saint, rather than to the other two gentlemen.

There is nothing ambiguous about the lake's function, though. Lying at the back door of Detroit, along the gilt-edged real estate of the Grosse Pointes, Lake St. Clair is one of the great recreation grounds of the Midwest. From summer, when its waters teem with the billowing sails of pleasure craft, to grey winter, when ice fishermen squat stolidly on its frozen surface, the lake is a haven for sportsmen. Pickerel drawn from its waters are a staple of area restaurants. The lake's shallow, sandy bottom also makes it a favored spot for swimmers. At the mouth of the St. Clair River is the area known as The Flats, a marshy, island-studded delta that offers exceptional boating. Amid all this recreational hubbub, the giant lake freighters make their stately way from Lake Huron toward Detroit, lumbering down their specially dredged channel in lordly indifference.

The St. Clair, like its sister river the Detroit, is one of the world's busiest stretches of water; and, like the Detroit, it is actually a strait. Despite its position on one of the continent's major highways of commerce, the river retains much of the beauty that delighted the explorers. In all the early journals, note is always taken of the forested scenery along the banks of the St. Clair. A parkway runs the entire length of the Canadian shore today, while on the Michigan side a succession of small towns with rich nautical histories lines the stream. The ship-building tradition is especially strong in Marine City, where the Ward family assembled one of the first great Michigan fortunes in their shipyards. They started with the steamer *Huron* in 1839 and soon put together a pioneer fleet that plied the waters between Detroit and Mackinac. St. Clair also had notable yards and Port Huron is credited with turning out 180 vessels between 1838 and 1908. In the old homes that front the water on both sides of the frontier, one can sense the long attachment to the river and the keen sense of its heritage.

The French were the first settlers in the St. Clair region and on the southern shore of the lake their influence remains strong. You can still hear the language spoken frequently in these small towns and even the mapmakers seem confused by the linguistic usage. One town, for example, appears on various maps as both Stoney Point and Point aux Roches.

There was a fort at the Lake Huron mouth of the St. Clair River as early as 1686 when Sieur du Lhut (who would later give his name in slightly amended form to the Minnesota city of Duluth at the head of Lake Superior) founded Fort St. Joseph. But aside from a few scattered settlements, there were no permanent villages established until after the War of 1812. The fur traders who came through the area first wanted to keep it unoccupied. Farmers would have only interfered with their trapping and commerce with the Indians. So the traders deliberately spread false stories about the barrenness of the land and settlers remained to the south. Only after the Americans established Fort Gratiot at Port Huron in 1813 did the area start to open up.

Sarnia, the largest Canadian city in the area—and indeed on the entire shoreline of Lake Huron—was settled in 1836. Sir John Colborne, lieutenant governor of Upper Canada, gave the city its distinct name. It's the Latin term for the English Channel island of Guernsey, where Colborne had been governor before his Canadian assignment.

There had been a few scattered earlier settlements on the Canadian shore. The earl of Selkirk tried to plant a colony of Highland Scots, Baldoon, a bit down the river near present-day Wallaceburg, but the settlement failed. Disciples of the British utopian Robert Owen founded an ideal community based on Owen's principles in 1829. It, too, went under.

After the Napoleonic Wars, many British army pensioners with titled names were drawn to the area by the promise of cheap land. They gave a certain tone to the young communities of Corunna and Sombra which they founded. It was not until 1858, however, that the area really began to grow and the catalyst was oil, not aristocracy. The strike was made to the east, in the vicinity of what is now Oil Springs. The first commercial well in North America touched off a boom and Sarnia quickly grew into a major refining center and port. Although the focus of Canada's oil industry has long since shifted west to Alberta, Sarnia remains the site of a pipeline terminal and a major petrochemical complex. The flames from its refineries are an after-dark attraction for sightseers.

Uncle Tom's Cabin

Josiah Henson already was sixty years old when he met the woman whose book would make him immortal. He was on a fund-raising trip to Massachusetts, trying to gain support for the vocational school he operated for fugitive slaves outside the village of Dresden, Ontario. The Anti-Slavery Society of Boston sought to assist him by publishing a pamphlet outlining Henson's life story. The brief history was read avidly by the woman writer, an ardent abolitionist. She became convinced that it contained the nucleus of a book, a story about the evil of slavery that would sear the American conscience. When Henson came to Andover, where she lived, she invited him to her home and had Henson recite the story of his life in fuller detail. By the time he finished, she knew she had her book. The woman was Harriet Beecher Stowe and the book was *Uncle Tom's Cabin*.

The novel began running in serial form two years later and became a national sensation, bitterly denounced in the South and read with indignation and horror in the North. The story was dramatized and touring companies took *Uncle Tom's Cabin* to playhouses all over the country. When President Lincoln later greeted Mrs. Stowe as "the little lady who started this big war," his overstatement was only marginal.

Mrs. Stowe never denied that her book, although incorporating many fictional devices and characters, was based mainly upon the life of Henson. He became something of a celebrity, lecturing throughout Canada and Britain and being greeted personally by Queen Victoria. Although many of the escaped slaves who lived with him returned to the United States at the end of the Civil War, Henson remained in Dresden and died there in 1883 at the age of ninety-four. His home, church, and some of the farm buildings from his educational facility, the British American Institute, remain on the site along with his grave. The buildings are open daily May through October, 10:00 to 6:00. There is an admission charge.

Henson was born into slavery on a farm in Charles County, Maryland. His father had his ear cut off and was sold to an

Alabama owner when he dared defend his wife against an over-seer. Henson never saw his father again, and shortly thereafter he and his mother were sold to a nearby plantation run by Isaac Riley. The new master was something of a ne'er-do-well and carouser. Once, while trying to defend him in a brawl, Henson had both his shoulder blades broken by an overseer. He never could raise his arms normally again. Riley eventually went bankrupt. In an effort to save his property, he asked Henson to take his family and eighteen other slaves to his brother's planta-tion in Kentucky. Although he had several chances to flee to the North en route, Henson carried out the mission.

Henson was now thirty-six years old. He had received a smattering of Christian education. During trips to the market he sought to improve himself by picking up the vocabulary and mannerisms of the white gentry. He was accepted as a preacher at the Episcopal Methodist Church and began urging his con-gregation to help him attain his freedom by purchase. He raised $275 in this manner and returned to Maryland to seek out his master, but Riley tricked him into signing a statement that dou-bled the purchase price and sent him back to Kentucky.

That settled the matter for Henson. Although he was de-voted to the Riley family, he saw his only alternative as escape. In 1830 he managed to get across the Ohio River to Indiana. Over the course of two months, hiding by day and traveling by night, he reached Sandusky, Ohio. A sympathetic lake captain took him to Buffalo and from there had him rowed across the Niagara River to Canada and freedom.

Henson's route was a shadowy predecessor to the Under-ground Railroad. By the time the Civil War began, this network of secret stations operated by antislavery Northerners was cred-ited with helping 75,000 escaped slaves reach safety in the cities of the North. After 1850 with the passage of the Fugitive Slave Act, the system was extended into Canada, where the slaves could finally outdistance pursuing Southerners.

The southeastern corner of Michigan became a focal point for all the routes leading from the South to freedom. Separated only by rivers from Canada and readily accessible from the slaveholding state of Kentucky, the area became the great terminus of the Railroad. The Finney Barn in downtown Detroit was famous as the last stop for escaping slaves before the final crossing into Canadian territory. They were then generally carried to Chatham, a hotbed of antislavery sentiment. It is believed, in fact, that the details of John Brown's raid on Harper's Ferry were planned at the First Baptist Church in that city during an 1858 abolitionist convention.

The Fugitive Slave Act outraged Michigan, which had a growing community of black freedmen in Detroit. When a group of Kentuckians entered the town of Marshall and tried to take an escaped slave back by force, the state jailed and fined

Josiah Henson's home, the original Uncle Tom's Cabin, is part of a museum complex in Dresden, Ontario. *Courtesy the* Detroit Free Press.

the pursuers. It was because of the intense antislavery feeling there, growing out of such incidents, that the key organizational meeting of the new Republican party was held in Jackson, Michigan.

Henson made several influential friends after entering Canada. In 1841 his friends managed to acquire 200 acres on the Sydenham River, north of Chatham, and formed a trade school for escaped slaves. The British American Institute gave the newcomers a rudimentary education and instructed them in trades like carpentry and smithing. Women were taught to cook and sew. The institute went bankrupt in the 1850s, and after emancipation there was no further use for its services. Henson, however, stayed on, preaching at the church on the institute grounds and occupying the home he had built there.

The site is now just west of the town of Dresden. A museum offers displays on Henson's life, the historical context of the slavery question, and items relating to the history of *Uncle Tom's Cabin*. Henson's church still stands, along with some agricultural buildings and a shack used to house newly arrived slaves. And, of course, there is also the wooden, two-story structure built in 1842 that was Henson's home—the original and genuine Uncle Tom's Cabin.

Cranbrook

It began as a picnic ground. At the turn of the century Bloom-field Hills was a farming area, a rural community connected by interurban rail and primitive road to the great city of Detroit, 18 weary, dusty miles away. Today it is one of the wealthiest places in America—a favored residential site for automotive executives and an address that announces its bearer has made it in Detroit. Even without its social cachet, its gently rolling, lake-dotted landscape was always a relief from the flatness of the surrounding area.

When George Booth first saw the place it reminded him of his native village in the Kentish countryside of England. Booth had married the daughter of James Scripps, who had made a fortune in publishing the *Detroit News,* one of the first mass circulation evening dailies in the country. Booth had succeeded his father-in-law as publisher and in 1904 was looking for a location for a summer home, away from the cares of the city. That's when he found the 300-acre site that would become Cranbrook, the name of his birthplace far away.

The Booths moved into a remodeled farmhouse at first, but as their friends discovered the charms of the hills, a more per-manent abode was felt to be suitable. Booth retained architect Albert Kahn, who was busily inventing the design of the mod-ern factory for Henry Ford at the time, and commissioned him to build a residence. It would be called Cranbrook House.

The mansion, built over a period of ten years, remained the home of the Booths until their deaths in the late 1940s. It is built atop a rise in an area then regarded as unspeakably iso-lated. It was fairly common for the Booths and their house guests to be stranded during winter storms for days at a time. A horse and carriage, supplemented by a Pierce-Arrow automo-bile, transported guests from the mile-distant interurban station to the house.

In 1918, the Booths built a meeting house near an adjacent brook for informal community religious gatherings and then began to use it as a school for neighborhood children. This arrangement became Brookside School in 1922, an elementary day school and the first of the Cranbrook institutions. By now the Booths had begun to envision much more than a picnic ground on their property. They began to plan an educational and cultural center as a community for artists and scholars who would find inspiration among the lovely hills. In 1927 they created the Cranbrook Foundation to ensure the survival of their dream beyond the span of their lives. Half a century later the dream is thriving.

You first sense Cranbrook's uniqueness on the approach from the south, through the suburbs from Detroit on Cranbrook Road. Near the intersection of Lone Pine Road, the scenery abruptly changes from midwestern suburban to British bucolic as the Gothic outline of Christ Church rises above the trees. This is the religious edifice that grew out of the simple services at the meeting house. Built between 1925 and 1929 by craftsmen employing contemporary motifs within the medieval framework, the church contains both modern works of art and ecclesiastical pieces from every century since the eleventh. It is open daily from 8:00 to 5:00. Carillon concerts are given every Sunday from May through September at 4:00.

If you continue a short distance along Cranbrook Road, east of the institution grounds, you will reach the site of Brookside School, which has incorporated the original meeting house into its buildings.

Return to Lone Pine Road. Opposite Christ Church is the entry gate to the Cranbrook grounds. This splendid tract of hills, gardens, and lakes is a favorite strolling place for Detroit residents on summer and autumn weekends. The forty acres of gardens are open daily, 1:00 to 5:00, Memorial Day to October; weekends only for the remainder of May. There is an admission charge.

Cranbrook House itself is not one of Kahn's more notable works. It was built over too long a time in too disjointed a fashion to contain a unity of style. But the interior is warm and contains many mementoes of the Booths. Tours are given the fourth Sunday of each month, 1:00 to 3:00; admission charge.

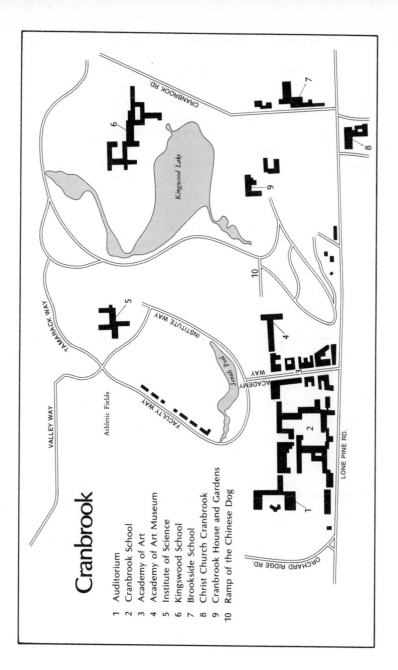

Cranbrook

1 Auditorium
2 Cranbrook School
3 Academy of Art
4 Academy of Art Museum
5 Institute of Science
6 Kingwood School
7 Brookside School
8 Christ Church Cranbrook
9 Cranbrook House and Gardens
10 Ramp of the Chinese Dog

VALLEY WAY

TAMARACK WAY

Athletic Fields

FACULTY WAY

INSTITUTE WAY

ACADEMY WAY

Jonah Pond

LONE PINE RD.

ORCHARD RIDGE RD.

Kingwood Lake

CRANBROOK RD.

After exploring the house and its surrounding fountains and terraces, make your way behind the building to the lake. Across the water is Kingswood School, a secondary educational facility for girls, built on what was once a stand of oak trees known as Angley Wood. The lake is a delightful corner of Cranbrook, with its flocks of ducks and swans searching for handouts from visitors. Complete the circuit of the house to a tree-lined promenade, called the Ramp of the Chinese Dog. This lovely pathway leads up a gentle incline from Cranbrook House to another slight rise to the west. The Booths had at first considered this area for the site of their home but it was then regarded as impossibly remote. Today the main structures of the Cranbrook institutions are situated upon the hill.

The design of Cranbrook School made the American reputation of Finnish-born architect Eliel Saarinen. He joined with Swedish sculptor Carl Milles and other artists to plan and decorate the school, the adjoining Academy of Art, and their surroundings. The graceful structures, set off by capacious fountains with their fanciful statues of animals and nymphs, make a walk around the area one of the most enchanting excursions in Detroit. The school itself is not open to the public. The Cranbrook Academy of Art Museum, however, featuring changing exhibitions by its talented students, is open from 1:00 to 5:00, except on Monday. There is an admission charge.

The nearby Institute of Science is a more recent addition to the Cranbrook group, opening in 1938. It is highly regarded for its displays on mineralogy and geology and for its planetarium. The institute is open 10:00 to 5:00 on weekdays, 1:00 to 9:00 on Saturday, and 1:00 to 5:00 on Sunday. Planetarium shows are given at 4:00 on Wednesday and 2:00, 3:00, and 4:00 on Saturday and Sunday, with an additional 7:30 evening show on Saturday. There is an admission charge.

General Motors Technical Center

Charles Kettering once referred to it, in his roughly affectionate way, as "an intellectual golf course." But he also called it a "telescope of tomorrow" and that is probably closer to the mark in describing the sprawling General Motors Tech Center in the Detroit suburb of Warren.

Present time ends at the gates to this place. Inside, everything is focused on the future: the cars you'll be driving five years from today, the roads you'll be driving on in twenty, the fuel you'll be driving with in twenty-five. That's what is being developed in this campuslike research center.

The innovative Kettering, who headed GM's Research Division, was chosen to give a main address at the opening of the center in 1956. He tried to explain the significance of what was going to happen there:

> The inventor fails 9,999 times and if he succeeds once, he is in. . . . It may be fifty or sixty years sometimes before an idea develops into a product, but if we will recognize that . . . the future is the greatest natural asset we have.

Since then, the ideas and the products have flowed from the GM Tech Center, from lightweight aluminum engines to pollution control devices to remote control heart catheters. Some of them, like automatic highway controls and single-stick devices to operate acceleration, braking, and steering, have remained in the labs. Many others, however, have been an accepted part of the highway scene for years since they emerged from the center.

The GM Tech Center with its artificial lake, splashing fountains, glazed brick facades, and adjacent green belt presents a striking contrast to the monolithic GM corporate headquarters in Detroit. The Detroit facility's repetitious rows of windows and columns represent the mechanical dependability that the automakers were content with in the early days of the industry. The Tech Center illustrates the change in style that came over the automotive world in the intervening years, changes pioneered in no small part by GM.

The giant corporation, once the largest in America, was formed in 1908. William Durant, the energetic head of Buick Motors, merged his company with Oldsmobile and within a year also had acquired Cadillac and Oakland Motors (which would become Pontiac). Chevrolet was added in 1911 and gave the new company an important entree to the low-cost end of the market. Durant wanted to buy out Henry Ford, too, but New York bankers, dubious about the future of this odd industry, refused to give him sufficient credit to meet the $8-million asking price. By the 1920s, GM was worth that much in multiples.

The company suspected, though, that business could be even better if somehow the American consumer could be persuaded to buy a new car more frequently. Ford had set the industry pattern with his Model T. The same car was turned out year after year because it was far less expensive than retooling each year for an altered product. When Ford finally unveiled the new Model A, it was an event of national importance and excited enormous curiosity. At about the same time, a GM executive on a visit to the west coast met Harley Earl, a young man who had set up a business designing custom cars for Hollywood celebrities. Earl was invited to come to Detroit and design a car for GM. The result was the 1927 LaSalle, a car that created a sensation with its innovative lines.

By the 1930s, GM executives had become convinced that annual model changeovers held the key to expanded sales. Great advertising campaigns were dreamed up, helping to create a phenomenon that came to be known by its critics as "planned obsolescence." A new car every two years became one of the country's firmest middle-class traditions. GM learned how to maximize profits by adapting three or four basic chassis designs to fit the models of all five of its automotive divisions.

In 1938, though, something more substantial occurred. Earl, by then vice president in charge of design, supervised the construction of the first GM prototype car, the Y-Job. It wedded the work of the design and research divisions in a vehicle that could model both technical advances and styling possibilities—the core of what goes on now at the Tech Center. The Y-Job contained such innovations as power windows, power convertible top, concealed headlights, and continuous fender strips.

The most fruitful of the prototypes drawn up by Earl's staff was the LeSabre of 1951. The name was eventually incorporated into the Buick line. Some of the features it pioneered were the panoramic windshield, deep-dish steering wheel, bucket seats, a lower center of gravity, and tail fins—those fondly remembered relics of the 1950s.

The prototypes of tomorrow's car can be seen at the Tech Center today. The facility is located on Mound Road north of Twelve Mile Road, about 3 miles east of Interstate 75. The one-hour bus tour of the complex visits the design center and includes a look at some actual models and how they are created. The tour also stops at exhibits of technical and styling advances that originated here. Innovations occur in fields other than automotive, too. The curiosity of GM's scientists does not end at curbside, and they are encouraged to follow concepts and find where they lead. Although the place lacks an assembly line (the popular symbol of the industry), the bus ride offers an informative and compelling look at the insides of this enormous operation. The tours are free and are given from Memorial Day to Labor Day, on the hour, from 10:00 to 5:00.

Other Things to See

[1]   The Detroit Zoological Park, which is actually located in the Oakland County suburb of Royal Oak, has long been one of the most innovative such institutions in the country. Its cageless exhibits, with animals grouped by continents in displays of their natural habitats, are spread over 122 landscaped acres, connected by a miniature train. Animal shows are held periodically in the Holden Amphitheater. The zoo is open 10:00 to 5:00, Monday to Saturday, mid-May to mid-September; Sundays, 9:00 to 6:00. The rest of the year it is open 10:00 to 4:00, except for Monday and Tuesday. There is an admission charge and an additional charge for parking. It's on West Ten Mile Road at Ridge Road.

[2]   Pontiac was named for the great Ottawa chief who led a massive rebellion against the British and lived in the area. Its name is more closely associated today, however, with automobiles. The General Motors Corporation Truck and Coach plant here offers tours on Thursday at 1:30 P.M.; but they are discontinued during periods of model changeover. For current information, call 857-4287. The plant is located at 660 South Boulevard.

[3]   The Silverdome Stadium, with its air-supported roof and 80,000 seats, is the home of Detroit's professional football and basketball teams, the Lions and Pistons. Tours are given from Tuesday through Sunday, 10:00 to 4:00, except when a Lions game or other day event is being held there. The dome is on Michigan 59 at Opdyke Road, east of Pontiac. There is an admission charge.

[4]   When the big automotive money started pouring into Detroit, it built some homes of surpassing grandeur. One of them was Meadowbrook Hall, near Rochester, the home of John Dodge's widow (later the wife of Alfred G. Wilson). The 100-room Tudor mansion, built in 1926, is a storehouse of artistic treasures and an architectural showplace in its own right. It's located off Walton Boulevard on the Oakland University campus. Open Sunday, 1:00 to 5:00. In July and August, it is also open from 10:30 to 5:00, Tuesday through Saturday. There is an admission charge.

Lake St. Clair

Keyed to *Other Things To See*

[5] The Grosse Pointes, the suburbs whose names are synonymous with established money in the automotive world, run along Lake St. Clair north from its junction with the Detroit River at the Detroit city limits. A fine drive through the area can be made by following East Jefferson Avenue and Lake Shore Drive from Grosse Pointe Park through Grosse Pointe Shores.

[6] Mineral baths made Mt. Clemens a popular nine-teenth-century spa. Although most of the baths are closed now, and the town is a booming Detroit suburb and county seat, its proximity to the lake still brings a resort trade. Metropolitan Beach, a 550-acre park with a mile-long beachfront on the lake, is 4 miles east of town. There is an entry charge.

[7] St. Clair is the most pleasant of the little towns that line the Michigan shore of the St. Clair River. The old shipbuilding center has completely remodeled its downtown section to form a 1,500-foot-long boardwalk along the river, supposedly the longest in the world facing fresh water. The grassy slopes above the boardwalk are an ideal place for watching the lake traffic go by and the town is a favorite weekend destination for Detroiters. Many of them stay at the St. Clair Inn, a good hotel and restaurant at the northern end of the boardwalk.

[8] Port Huron's position at the head of the St. Clair River has always made it a place of military and navigational importance. There was a French fort on the site as early as 1686 and the Fort Gratiot Light, built in 1829, is one of the oldest on the Great Lakes. The Museum of Arts and History, at 1115 Sixth Street, gives a good account of local history. It is open Wednesday through Sunday, 1:00 to 4:30. The city really comes alive each July when the Port Huron-Mackinac Sail Race begins here. On the eve of the race, downtown Port Huron becomes a street carnival as sailors and sightseers celebrate the coming event. The race itself is a thrilling spectacle, one of the top sporting events in Michigan. The date varies annually.

[9] The Blue Water Bridge connects Port Huron with Sarnia, Ontario, and commands dramatic views of the mouth of Lake Huron. Opened in 1938, the bridge is 8,021 feet long.

There is a charge for vehicles but pedestrians may walk across free.

[10]   Canatara Park offers Lake Huron beaches right in Sarnia, with a small children's farm besides. The city's most unusual attraction, though, is Chemical Valley, just south of town on Highway 40. A drive through this petrochemical complex by day is awesome enough; but at night, with its flares lighting the sky for miles around, it is a scene from the *Inferno.*

[11]   The St. Clair Parkway runs along the river from Sarnia to Wallaceburg and is an outstanding scenic drive. Ontario has set aside much of the land for public parks. As a result, the traveler can stop every few miles for a view of the river traffic, a picnic, or a swim. And the views as he drives, for the most part, are unobstructed.

[12]   The *Imperial Hamilton,* a veteran Lakes oil tanker that was crippled in port in Sarnia by an explosion in 1961, was saved from the scrap heap by a sailing enthusiast. Its pilot house was brought to the river shore at Corunna, where it remains as a museum of its own history and that of the area. It is open from May to mid-October, Monday through Saturday, 10:00 to 5:00; Sunday, 2:00 to 5:00. There is an admission charge.

[13]   Walpole is the largest island in the St. Clair River delta, known as The Flats. It is now an Indian preserve and offers fine hunting, fishing, and swimming at public beaches. Highbanks Park on its northern tip is a beauty spot. The island is accessible by causeway from the St. Clair Parkway or by ferryboat from Algonac, Michigan.

[14]   Other ferryboats in the vicinity link Port Lambton, Ontario, with Roberts Landing, Michigan, and Sombra, Ontario, with Marine City, Michigan.

[15]   Wallaceburg is an especially pleasant old town built at the forks of the Sydenham River. A well-kept park overlooks the forks and several bridges across the narrow river also afford views of the town. There are some fine vintage business structures and churches on James Street, Wellington Street, and the side streets branching from them.

[16]   The first oil boom in America was touched off in the late 1850s near what is now the village of Oil Springs. They still take a little black gold from the ground here, but the biggest reminder of those days is the Oil Museum of Canada, just south of the town, on the site of the first commercial well. The displays lack a coherent historical development but there is plenty of information scattered among the exhibits on the industry and its local history. The museum is open from late May through October, 10:00 to 6:00; admission charge.

[17]   Mitchell's Bay is one of the top pan fishing areas of Lake St. Clair. The area around the little French-Canadian hamlet has been turned into a marine park, with full facilities for all water recreation, by the St. Clair Parkway Commission.

[18]   Chatham has long been known as a city of maples, a tree especially dear to Canadians. One of the best places to enjoy the foliage is in Tecumseh Park—a sprawling recreation grounds in the heart of the city with a bandstand, gardens, pools, and lawn bowling, overlooking the Thames River. Nearby is the Chatham-Kent Museum, at 59 William Street North, which houses a good regional collection. It is open Tuesday, Thursday, Saturday, and Sunday, 2:00 to 5:00, from May through September; the rest of the year, Sunday openings are only on the first and third week of the month. Free.

Side Trips

Thamesville, 16 miles northeast of Chatham, is where the retreating British and Indian forces tried to make their stand against the pursuing Americans on the retreat from Detroit in 1813. The Americans won a smashing victory at the Battle of the Thames, 2 miles east of town, and among the slain was the great Shawnee leader, Tecumseh. A memorial marks the spot on Highway 2.

Two miles farther east is the site of Fairfield, a Moravian mission that was wiped out by the American forces who suspected the sect of aiding the Indians. The mission was reestablished on the far side of the river after the war and a museum there relates the history of Fairfield and the Moravians. It is open Monday through Saturday, 9:00 to 5:00; Sunday, 1:30 to 7:00.

State and Provincial Parks along the Lake

Metropolitan Beach—4 miles southeast of Mt. Clemens, Michigan, is operated by the Huron-Clinton Metropark Authority. It offers swimming and all water sports, a par-three golf course, shuffleboard, tennis, archery, picnicking, and roller-skating. No camping.

Algonac—2 miles north of Algonac, Michigan, is a 981-acre site with boating facilities and picnicking but no swimming. There are 390 campsites.

The St. Clair Parkway Commission operates a whole series of small day-use parks along the St. Clair River between Sarnia and Wallaceburg. Most have picnicking facilities and many of them have boating and swimming. There is camping at Cathcart Park and Lambton Cundick Park, both just north of Sombra.

The Presque Isle Lighthouse, located between Alpena and Rogers City, Michigan, has stood at the mouth of Presque Isle Harbor since 1840. *Courtesy the* Detroit Free Press.

6

The Thumb to Thunder Bay

North of Port Huron the face of Michigan changes abruptly. The freeways become country roads, and the bustling cities turn to villages. Commerce is a freighter glimpsed far out on Lake Huron. Industry is a dairy herd grazing on bluffs far above the water. It is not yet the North country, but it is no longer the industrialized belt, either.

This is the Thumb, a sort of threshhold to the North. It is flat country, heavily Germanic, and utterly tranquil. Most of Michigan's Lake Huron shore is like this all the way to Thunder Bay, the last major indentation of the lake before the Straits of Mackinac. At the peak of the tourist season, when the Lake Michigan shoreline is packed to capacity and beyond, the Huron side remains peaceful. When every motel room and campsite in the North is taken, there is almost always room along the Huron shore. The dramatic Lake Michigan dunes drew crowds from the time the tourist industry began in the state, late in the nineteenth century, and for the most part that's where the crowds have remained. Fashionable resorts followed the railroads and the highways up the western shore. Huron, with a few exceptions, remained far from the mainstream; and no place is farther than the Thumb.

A quick glance at the map will explain its name. The Lower Peninsula of Michigan is shaped like a mitten, with the outline of Saginaw Bay carving out a perfect thumb. It is such a placid area today that it is hard to associate it with epic disasters. But fire and storm have taken their toll here and shaped the history of the Thumb.

Like all of Michigan north of Detroit, it began to develop with the lumbering industry in the mid-nineteenth century. Its stands of white pine were fairly well depleted by 1871, however, and the area slowly began converting to farming.

That summer had been unusually warm and dry, and the hot weather held into October. On the eighth day of the month, far to the west, a fire broke out that would destroy the young city of Chicago. But the blaze did not end there. Carried by a fierce western gale, sparks swept around the southern end of Lake Michigan and into the swamp country. The fire began moving across the state of Michigan like a red tide. By the time it reached the Thumb, nothing could stop it. In the counties of Sanilac and Huron, the destruction was appalling. An area forty miles square was burned out in these two counties.

The fire all but destroyed the remnants of lumbering in the Thumb and the conversion to agriculture accelerated. Then, ten years less one month later, the fire came again. This time it was the most devastating forest fire in the history of the state. The same Thumb areas that had been hardest hit by the first blaze were burned clean again in 1881. By the time the fire burned itself out on the lakeshore, 125 people were dead, 3,400 buildings had been destroyed, and the damage was placed at two million dollars. The smoke billowed across the lake and darkened the sky as far away as Collingwood, Ontario. A total of 1,800 square miles was blackened. Families fleeing for the safety of the lake were separated in the smoky blackness and lost their bearings; many died running desperately back into the flames. It was the first national disaster in which the American Red Cross was called in for relief.

The land healed, but in 1913 another disaster came, this time by water. Again the destruction was carried on gale winds, the Great Storm of November 9. A historical marker has been placed on a bluff along Michigan 25 south of Port Sanilac. It was in this area that the greatest losses were recorded. Ten ships went down in the blow and 235 sailors lost their lives, the most terrible toll of any storm in Lakes history. Eight of the ships were lost on Huron, most of them in the narrow part of the lake above Port Huron.

The weather bureau had issued severe gale warnings earlier in the week, but November had been so mild that no one could believe anything would come of the forecast. Even on the morning of the storm it was temperate and calm. As the morning progressed, though, the temperature plummeted and snow started to blow in from the west. By midday, Detroit and Cleveland were buried and scores of smaller cities were cut off totally. The winds raged for sixteen hours before passing beyond the Lakes.

In the calm of the following morning, observers on the shore near Port Huron noticed a strange floating object on the lake horizon. A telescope was found. The viewers, with mounting apprehension, could see it was a capsized hull. Rescue boats were unable to find the ship's identity since thick ice covered the capsized vessel's nameplates. From Canada came chilling reports of bodies washing ashore. They wore life vests from several ships—*Wexford, Regina, James Carruthers, Charles S. Price.* Slowly it was becoming clear that a disaster of terrible proportions had occurred on the icy lake.

Ships that had survived made their way to port with harrowing tales: the water had been a seething mass, thirty-five-foot waves striking three at a time and running opposite the seventy-mile-an-hour winds; all familiar landmarks had vanished in the blowing snow; no one was able to fix a position.

The capsized vessel was identified as the *Price*. It was a shocking discovery for the ship was only three years old and was fully equipped with the latest safety devices. It was 9,000 **tons,** 524 feet in length. An even greater shock was to come.

The *Carruthers,* launched only the previous May, had also gone down. Seven of the eight ships that were lost were less than ten years old. If these ships had gone down, nothing could have survived the storm.

The grim task of identifying the bodies continued in Canada. Eventually, all but five of the dead were claimed. The remaining victims were buried in Goderich under a memorial obelisk.

A mystery remained that was never to be solved. One of the dead had been identified as a crew member of the *Price;* but he had washed ashore wearing a life preserver from the *Regina.* What had happened? Did the two ships collide? Did they pass so close that equipment passed from one to the other? No one who knew the answer survived the Great Storm.

Huron National Forest

When the first Europeans came, almost all of Michigan was forest. Early travelers through the Saginaw Valley, including the French historian Alexis de Tocqueville, were overwhelmed at this wooded empire, so thickly treed that even at noon in midsummer the forest floor was dark. There was beauty here, and there was also wealth. More riches than would ever be taken from the goldfields of California or the Klondike. Fortunes that would swell to some of the largest ever accumulated in America and that later would provide the starting capital for the automobile industry. But along with all this came the ravishing of the land, a destruction so enormous as to be almost mindless. So great was the despoiling that only in recent decades, in preserves like the Huron National Forest, has some of the land been repaired. The economy of many areas of northern Michigan never fully recovered from the end of the lumbering era.

At first, the trees were only a nuisance. Except for the dune country of the extreme southwestern corner, Michigan was one huge forest—95 percent of the land by some estimates. The early settlers were interested in farms, though, and the stands of trees on their property were simply felled and burned. It was only in the 1850s that the wealth standing all around was recognized.

There had been sawmills in the Saginaw Valley as early as 1782 and many communities engaged in small scale lumbering to serve local needs and the Detroit market. In 1819 the government purchased, from the Chippewas, the Huron shoreline as far north as Alpena and the exploration and surveying of the vast tract began. David Ward, a member of a Detroit family that had grown rich on their Marine City shipyards, conducted the survey. For his services he was given one-fourth of the land. It was land full of white pine and Norway pine. It might just as well have been full of diamonds.

Two movements of major significance were going on in America at about the same time Ward was taking title to his land. The pine forests of Maine, which had served the country's lumber needs since colonial times, were exhausted. New sources of wood were needed immediately. Simultaneously, the westward movement had spilled onto the prairie lands west of Chicago and there was a desperate need for building material in that tree-starved region. Both of these needs converged upon the rich, virgin timberlands of Michigan and for the next four decades the boom was on.

In 1872, 2.5 billion feet of pine lumber were taken from the state. Eleven years later it totaled 4 billion feet. In the peak decades of the 1880s, it is estimated that 3.5 billion feet a year were shipped out of Michigan. There were 1,649 lumbering installations in the state, $39 million in capital investment, 24,000 people employed, and a $52 million total valuation of lumber. In 1888 the amount of sawed lumber coming out of the Saginaw Valley alone would have made a sidewalk of two-inch planks, four feet wide, that would have reached around the world four times. In Cheboygan, mills working twenty-four hours a day piled up a sawdust mountain sixty feet high over ten acres in area. They used the sawdust in Alpena to fill in the swamps, grade the streets, extend the beach into the lake, and form piers to load the cut lumber onto ships. In Bay City, the mills crowded the entire length of the Saginaw River through the town.

The first lumbering operations grew up along the rivers that flowed into the Lakes—the Saginaw and Au Sable on the Lake Huron side, and the Grand and Muskegon on the Lake Michigan shore. The logs were floated down the streams and cut up at the mill boomtowns. Saginaw was the greatest of them, but others were not far behind in size and wealth. Before long, the cutting operations had penetrated far inland, and in 1877 the first narrow gauge railroad was built to carry the logs to water.

In 1890 there were 700 logging camps and 2,000 sawmills in the state. There were also 1.8 million acres of waste pine land in the Lower Peninsula. Along the Au Sable River, the chief stream of the Huron National Forest, the total log flow that year was half of what it had been five years before. In many areas the forests had been picked clean. Although there was some transfer to hardwood lumbering, within another twenty years Michigan had fallen from first place to tenth among the states in lumber production. The center of the industry moved on to Minnesota and the Pacific Northwest, leaving behind a colorful history and lore, a great many wealthy men, and a devastated state.

The Lumberman's Monument is a nine-foot bronze sculpture erected to honor the memory of early Michigan loggers. *Courtesy Michigan Tourist Council.*

Arbor Day had been proclaimed in Michigan as far back as 1876 by the governor. It seemed then to make about as much sense as holding a Sand Day on the Sahara. The state forestry commission issued periodic warnings of the damage that was being done but had no powers to do anything about it. In 1903, as the boom petered out, a state forestry reserve was established. Eight years later legislation was passed allowing land turned over to reforestation to be exempt from taxation.

The Huron National Forest was established in 1909 along the banks of the bruised Au Sable River. Today it is a 417,000-acre facility that spreads across five counties. The Au Sable runs through it on its final sixty miles before emptying into Lake Huron. There are 110,000 acres of plantation in the forest. A total of 550,000 feet of sawlogs and 70,000 cords of pulpwood are taken from it annually. The land is a renewable resource if properly managed, rather than savaged.

There are fifteen recreation areas in the forest, with fishing offered at all but one, and swimming on eight inland lakes. There are also 61 picnic sites and 206 campsites. A self-guiding auto tour explains what has been done to this onetime wasteland to return it to production and recreational use.

The Au Sable is a favorite river for canoeists and an outstanding trout stream, as well. Near the center of the forest at Mack Lake is a special habitat area for the rare Kirtland's warbler. The land is set aside to protect this songbird which nests only in this portion of Michigan. A census in 1977 revealed that there were 200 singing males remaining, but that was up from a 1974 low of 167 birds. Tours of the nesting area are given from ranger stations in Mio and Grayling. No other entry is permitted between mid-May and mid-July.

The chief attraction in the forest, though, is the monument to the lumbermen. Bigger than life at nine feet in height, the group of three bronze figures was erected in 1932. It honors the men who cleared the forests and made possible the settlement of the prairies. They did not set the policies that laid the land waste, after all. Their job was to get the timber, and they did it extraordinarily well. The figures represent a timber cruiser (who scouted the land for likely new stands), a tree feller, and a river driver. At the monument is a scenic overlook across the Au Sable; the auto tour also begins here. The monument is located about 13 miles northwest of East Tawas and the same distance west of Oscoda on marked, national forest roads.

There are ranger stations at East Tawas and Harrisville on Lake Huron, and at Mio in the interior. The forest headquarters is in Cadillac.

Huron City

The town has been gone for almost a century; but it refuses to die. Instead it lives on as a memorial to its settlers and to an eloquent minister who gave it new life. The reason for Huron City's existence ended in 1881 with the second great forest fire that swept across the Thumb, effectively ending the lumbering industry in the area. The town's founder, Langdon Hubbard, had intended it as a lake port for a 29,000-acre tract of timberlands he had acquired. A mile-long dock was constructed on the lakefront at the mouth of Willow Creek, and two sawmills there produced 80,000 feet of lumber a day.

The fire ended all that. Hubbard turned some of his land over to homesteaders but his little town had already started to wither away. By the turn of the century it was just a shell. All that remained was the general store, the hulk of the hotel, the Hubbards' rambling summer home "Seven Gables," and the church. It was the latter structure that was Huron City's salvation.

Hubbard's daughter Annabel had married a young Yale University professor, William Lyon Phelps. His field was English literature, but he was also an ordained minister. Dr. Phelps had a knack for translating sophisticated theological concepts into readily understandable sermons, couched in everyday language. Freed from jargon and pietistic obscurities, Dr. Phelps's sermons were extremely effective lectures, illluminating passages from the Gospels with applications to contemporary life.

He and his wife spent their summers at Seven Gables in the ghost town. In the early 1920s, Dr. Phelps began the practice of delivering a sermon each Sunday at 3:00 P.M. in the little church. The structure seated only 250 people, and soon the crowds that showed up to hear the sermons were standing in the aisles and along the back wall. The church was enlarged, then enlarged again until it could hold a congregation of 1,000—more than had ever lived in the area when Huron City was booming. The fame of Dr. Phelps's summertime sermons soon spread throughout the state. On Sunday afternoons, motorists would find their way to the little church from nearby resort areas and farming towns. By the 1930s, when the roads had improved somewhat, families would make the long drive from Detroit to spend the Sabbath listening to Dr. Phelps and then return home by night.

He became known as Dr. Billy and the church in Huron City, "the visible church in the invisible town" in his words, was a sentimental landmark. Eddie Guest, whose poems for the *Detroit Free Press* were reprinted around the country, fired off a tribute to his friend, Dr. Phelps:

> There is no gothic architecture to attract the passerby,
> There is no dome or massive steeple towering far into the
>   sky . . .
> But of all God's holy places, there is none holier to me
> Than that church at Huron City where the service starts at
>   three.

In 1937, Dr. Phelps died and the little town was quiet once more. This time it was the granddaughter of the founder who would not let it die. Carolyn Hubbard Lucas felt Huron City merited preservation as a museum of the lumber era and of the life of Dr. Phelps. With the establishment of the William Lyon Phelps Foundation, Huron City began its final transformation into a museum town. Today, there is a total of five historic buildings open to the public. There is also a modern museum structure which serves as an introduction to the area and contains personal mementoes of Dr. Phelps. Seven Gables also remains, although it is not open to tourists.

The old inn has been refurbished in its mid-Victorian appearance, with one large room redone as a schoolroom of the period would have looked. A settler's cabin, built sometime in the 1820s, has been moved here from elsewhere in the county. It illustrates the rigors of life on what was then an isolated frontier. The coast guard station from Point Aux Barques, at the very tip of the Thumb, was moved here and restored in 1962 after seventy-five years of service. It contains nautical exhibits and displays of the Coast Guard's rescue operations on the lake.

A generally good historical display on the lumbering era has been set up in the general store, a short walk north of the village on the far side of Willow Creek. The store itself is outfitted as it would have been in a pioneer community.

The church stands, too. It is silent now, as it has been since Dr. Phelps's final sermon, but it is still a very visible presence in this still visible town.

The Huron City museum is located on a spur road off Michigan 25, between Port Hope and Port Austin. It is open from July 1 to Labor Day, 10:30 to 5:30; Sundays, noon to 5:00. There is an admission charge.

Presque Isle Lighthouse

A few myths die hard. That's because they are so appealing that by all rights they should be true. Just because history did not see fit to produce the facts to match the story seems a pretty poor excuse for demolishing a pleasant tale.

Such is the case of the old Presque Isle Lighthouse on the Lake Huron shore. It is located east of U.S. 23 on county roads, between Alpena and Rogers City. It has occupied its dramatic position at the mouth of Presque Isle Harbor since 1840. It served the function for which it was built for only thirty of those years, though, and since 1959 it has been a museum.

Over the years, the traditional tale evolved: the old light was either surveyed or built by Jefferson Davis who, in another twenty years, would become the president of the Confederacy. There seemed to be two pieces of information, both somewhat flimsy, on which the story was based. Equipment discovered on the site from the nineteenth century and presumably used in construction bore the inscription "J. Davis." And it was known that Davis did much of his U.S. Army service on the Wisconsin frontier. So, according to the story, Davis had been instructed by the government to find a likely site for a new light along the Huron shore and then to supervise the construction. It's nice to think of the future Confederate statesman roaming the Michigan coastline and then building this sturdy lighthouse, which has worn the years so well.

Unfortunately, there are quite a number of holes in the story. For one thing, Davis was not an engineer; it seems unlikely that even an institution like the army would entrust such a mission to an officer with absolutely no technical qualifications. For another, the records show that construction of the light was carried out by one Jeremiah Moors of Detroit. And for a third, Davis resigned from the army in 1835, three years before the lighthouse even had reached the planning stage. At the time it was built he was living on his Mississippi plantation.

The Presque Isle light really doesn't need the spirit of Jefferson Davis to make it a worthwhile attraction—although the old myth still turns up now and then in tourist brochures and newspaper stories. The fact is that Presque Isle Harbor was well known to military vessels, which frequently put in to cut hardwood for fuel. The harbor had been a landmark since the early days of French exploration. Traders portaged across the narrow neck of land between Lake Huron and Grand Lake and they referred to it as "presque isle" or "almost an island." The government decided to mark the harbor with a lighthouse in 1838 and appropriated $5,000 for the project. A slightly elevated site above the fishing village was selected and by 1840 the construction was complete. Although Jeremiah Moors is not as illustrious a name as Jefferson Davis, his work is still a marvel. The walls are four feet thick and the steps hand-chiseled from stone. Moors built it to last for the government's $5,000. The view from the top is a pleasant panorama of the lake, harbor, and village.

In 1870 it was decided that a new light was needed to mark the coastline, rather than the harbor entrance, and the old light was decommissioned. The forty-foot tower and adjacent keeper's home were abandoned for the next sixty years. Then, in 1930, the Stebbins family of Lansing purchased the old curiosity as a vacation home. They restored it and finally opened it to the public as a museum.

The entrance to the old light is dramatic. A narrow road winds through thick woods from the highway. With thin shafts of light penetrating the dark pine forest, it is a fine evocation of a vanished era in the North, a good threshold for a historic setting. The Stebbins family furnished the keeper's house with antiques from the period of its activity, including several artifacts from area shipwrecks. The displays are intended to convey a sense of how the keeper's family lived, since the original articles have been irretrievably scattered. A few other items of historic interest are placed around the grounds and a pebbly beach leads down to the water. And, of course, there is the climb up the circular stairway to the light tower itself, a rare chance to get inside one of the most historic lights on the Lakes.

The Presque Isle Lighthouse is open from Memorial Day to October 31, 8:00 A.M. to 8 P.M.; admission fee.

Other Things to See

[1]   The village of Croswell was faced with the problem of bridging the Black River in 1905 to get people to the picnic grounds on the far side. The solution was a swinging bridge, a suspension footbridge that shimmies and wobbles for 139 feet across the river. It's perfectly safe, though, and an exciting way to start a picnic. There is no charge.

[2]   Port Sanilac made the transformation from busy logging town to picturesque resort village beautifully. Its harbor, constructed by the U.S. Army Corps of Engineers in 1951, is one of the finest on Lake Huron and it is interesting to walk out along the piers. There's also a restaurant and playground at the water's edge. A short distance away, along Lake Street, there are some fine old homes and a government lighthouse. A regional museum with interesting exhibits on the state's pioneer dairy industry is on Michigan 25 south of town. It is open Thursday through Sunday, mid-June to Labor Day, 1:00 to 4:30; weekends only, the rest of September. There is an admission charge.

[3]   Harbor Beach is another town that services the Thumb's busy resort trade. It has added significance as the birthplace of Frank Murphy, who went on to become mayor of Detroit, governor of Michigan, and a justice on the U.S. Supreme Court. Murphy is best remembered for his pioneering efforts in social welfare during the Depression and his handling of the great sitdown strike at the Flint General Motors plants in 1937. His birthplace and family law offices are a museum. Open every day except Monday, 1:00 to 5:00, mid-June to Labor Day; admission charge.

[4]   Michigan 25 is never very far from the lake on its entire course around the Thumb. It is an especially scenic drive between Port Austin and Caseville, with views of Saginaw Bay and its islands and several roadside parks and turnouts.

[5]   The natural sandstone found at the top of the Thumb was just the thing for keeping the blades of the logging industry sharp. It was fashioned into grindstones at one of the area's

ports—later known as Grindstone City. Some of the old grind-wheels may still be seen on walks along the beach there.

[6]   Sebewaing is as sweet a town as they come. The Michigan Sugar Company refinery dominates the place and the surrounding area is one of the country's top beet sugar regions. Sebewaing celebrates with an annual Sugar Festival, usually held in early July.

[7]   Much of the timber money flowed into Bay City, where the lumber barons tried to outdo each other in building elaborate homes along Center Street. In the midst of this flavorful Victorian district, the Museum of the Great Lakes has displays on the history of the area. It is open 10:00 to 5:00 on weekdays, 1:00 to 5:00 on weekends; admission charge.

[8]   Center Street ends at the Saginaw River in downtown Bay City and its continuation is a pleasant waterside park. A pedestrian mall there, the Avenue of Flags, is lined with the national flags of every country that sails on the Great Lakes.

[9]   Pinconning is the center of Michigan's cheese industry. There is a festival celebrating the product each summer and shops offering a wide assortment of Michigan cheeses the year round.

[**10**]   Paul Bunyan's statue stands in the city park at Oscoda and each August a festival is held to honor the legendary lumberman. The town, which was almost completely destroyed by fire in 1911, is at the Lake Huron outlet of the Au Sable River. Cruises along the Au Sable into the adjacent Huron National Forest aboard the paddlewheeler *River Queen Number Two* are offered during the summer. The boat leaves from Foote Dam, 6 miles west of town along West River Road. Cruises depart at noon and 3:00 P.M. daily, from Memorial Day to Labor Day, and last for two hours. There is an additional Saturday twilight cruise at 6:00. There are also color cruises during the fall. Check locally for times. Reservations may be made by calling 517-739-7351 in Oscoda. Other trips depart from Five Channels Dam, 19 miles west of Oscoda on West River Road. Check locally for times.

[11]   Alpena, on the shores of Thunder Bay, was another

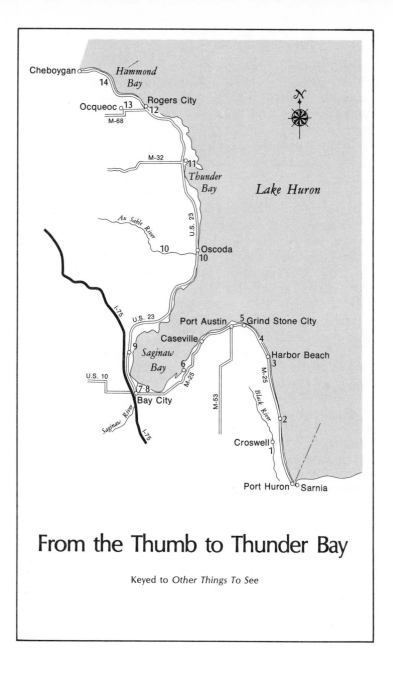

From the Thumb to Thunder Bay

Keyed to *Other Things To See*

of the lumbering boomtowns and the Jesse Besser Museum there examines its colorful past. It is located north of the business district on U.S. 23. The museum is open Monday through Friday, 9:00 to 5:00; Sunday, 1:00 to 5:00; closed Saturday. Free.

[12]   One of the greatest natural deposits of limestone in the world is situated near Rogers City. Since 1912 the U.S. Steel Corporation has shipped millions of tons of the high calcium-content stone from here for use in the steel, chemical, agricultural, and cement industries. Views of operations in the enormous quarry are available from a lookout south of town, off U.S. 23; the viewpoint is open daily, 9:00 to 5:00. A small museum houses displays that explain the mining operations; free.

[13]   There are several waterfalls in Michigan but they are concentrated in the Upper Peninsula. The one notable exception is Ocqueoc Falls, along the river of the same name. Its graceful upper and lower falls are joined by a park, off Michigan 68, 11 miles west of Rogers City.

[14]   North of Rogers City, U.S. 23 enters an especially scenic stretch along the Lake Huron shore. It passes along the shores of Hammond Bay and through a heavily wooded and undeveloped section of Presque Isle County. There are several roadside parks and turnouts on the route.

Side Trips

Ancient Indian rock carvings are in the process of being turned into a state park area in Sanilac County. They can be seen along the Cass River near the town of New Greenleaf in the northwestern corner of the county, about 45 miles northwest of Port Sanilac.

The Bavarian town of Frankenmuth is famed for its all-you-can-eat chicken dinners and its year-round exhibits of Christmas decorations at Bronner's. The showrooms are open 9:00 to 5:30, Monday through Saturday; 2:00 to 5:00 on Sunday; and until 9:00 P.M. on Thursday. The store is closed Saturday afternoons, January through April. The town holds a Bavarian Festival every June. It is 22 miles southeast of Bay City.

Michigan 13, between Bay City and Saginaw, is a pleasant drive through parkland along the Saginaw River.

Midland, 19 miles west of Bay City, is the home of the Dow Chemical Company—an enormous force in the city's cultural life. The Dow Gardens, with over six hundred species displayed on thirty-four acres, is open daily from 10:00 to 5:00; free. The Midland Center for the Arts is highlighted by the Great Hall of Ideas, a historical exhibit with particular reference to Michigan. Open Monday through Saturday, 9:00 to 5:00; Sunday, 1:00 to 5:00; free.

State Parks along the Lake

Lakeport—21 miles south of Port Sanilac, has complete water-sports facilities, swimming, and picnicking on 565 acres. There are 257 campsites.

Port Crescent—5 miles west of Port Austin, has swimming and boating on 209 acres. There are 180 campsites.

Albert E. Sleeper—5 miles east of Caseville, is a 963-acre facility with complete water sports and a concession store. There are 310 campsites.

Bay City—5 miles north of Bay City, has beaches, water sports, and a museum with natural history exhibits. There are 196 acres and 285 campsites.

Tawas Point—3 miles east of East Tawas, has a beach and picnic facilities on its 175 acres. There are 202 campsites.

Harrisville—1 mile south of Harrisville, has beaches, boating, and 229 campsites on its 94 acres.

P.H. Hoeft—5 miles north of Rogers City, is a 300-acre facility with beach, boating, and 146 campsites.

Framed by the contrasting skeletons of trees it has entombed and then uncovered, the Sleeping Bear Sand Dune towers some 460 feet above Lake Michigan. *Courtesy Michigan Tourist Council.*

7

The Traverse Bays

A soothing sound laps in with the waves along the shoreline of Grand and Little Traverse bays. It is the sound of money; Detroit automotive money and Chicago meat-packing money, established money and rip-roaring brand new money. This is some of the wealthiest resort property in America, maybe in the world. A Great Lakes Riviera. A Newport of the Midwest. However you phrase the comparison, the Lake Michigan shoreline north of Traverse City is one of the great playgrounds the country has to offer. For over a century it has attracted and held a discriminating summer clientele who can easily afford to spend their vacation wherever they choose; yet they always return here—joined by thousands of lesser means but with an equal appreciation of the land.

It is hilly country, unlike most of Michigan's Lower Peninsula, and large inland lakes nestle in the hills. In a few cases, like that of Charlevoix, a town may actually have two separate shorelines, one on Lake Michigan and another on an inland lake. Then there are the deep indentations of the two Traverse bays, the most distinctive features in this part of the Lakes. It all combines to make an almost ideal resort area.

The protected bays offer excellent sailing. The inland lakes are speckled with beaches. Since their temperatures are slightly higher than the water of Lake Michigan, one is able to take a dip without turning blue. The hills have made this an all-year resort area because luxurious ski installations keep the crowds coming during the season of deep snow.

Traverse City has become one of the state's fastest growing communities. In the space of two decades it was transformed from a small farming and resort town to the pivotal city of Michigan's north. Other cities in the area are experiencing the same phenomenon to a lesser degree. From all over the southern part of the state, people who first came here on vacation have decided to move in permanently. They feel they can escape the problems and frustrations of the great industrial cities of Michigan for a life they find more fulfilling and rewarding in every way but financially.

This was a favored land for the Indians of the north, too. Cross Village, the earliest settlement, was a great council center of the Ottawa. The French called the place L'Arbre Croche ("The Crooked Tree") after a great, gnarled fir that stood high upon the bluff and was clearly identifiable from the lake. A French Jesuit mission was established here in 1740 and was successful in its work among the Ottawa. Its existence proved especially fortuitous for the British successors in the area. After the fall of Fort Michilimackinac in Pontiac's Rebellion of 1763, the Ottawa of L'Arbre Croche rescued several British prisoners from the hands of the Chippewa. It was the first crack in Indian solidarity during the conspiracy and foreshadowed the disintegration of the uneasy tribal alliances forged by Pontiac.

As French influence faded, the mission settlement became known as Cross Village, because of a large white cross erected on the bluffs. Eventually, the mission was moved to the south and its named changed to Little Traverse. (The "Traverse" in the names of the bays refers to the crossing that had to be made there by French fur traders.) The new site, in turn, developed into Harbor Springs.

Across the bay in Petoskey, the mission of St. Francis Solanus was established in 1869. Six years later the railroad reached the tiny settlement, and in 1876 two Methodist clergymen established a summer camp in nearby Bay View, touching off a tourist boom that never has diminished.

Traverse City's road to prosperity was not nearly as smooth. The first permanent settlement in the area wasn't established until 1839, when a Presbyterian mission was built on the slender peninsula north of town (still called the Old Mission Peninsula). Under the name of Boardman, the city grew with the lumber boom of the late nineteenth century. By 1900 the big timber camps were on the move to the north and west, and the city seemed headed for decline and possible obliteration.

As the lumberjacks were leaving, a local farmer was experimenting in his fields with cherries. The harsh northern weather is tempered around Traverse City by the great bay; B. J. Morgan found it perfectly suited for growing red tart cherries, the kind that taste best in pies. His discovery filled the economic vacuum. Within a few years, Traverse City was the center of the most densely planted region of cherry orchards in the country. The springtime blossoms along the Old Mission Peninsula cover the landscape as a token of the area's permanent prosperity. The National Cherry Festival, held yearly in Traverse City on the first weekend after the Fourth of July, salutes the big crop.

The Leelenau Peninsula separates Grand Traverse Bay from Lake Michigan. It is also rich orchard country, with resorts sprinkled along its shore. The spectacular Sleeping Bear Dune, now part of a National Lakeshore, is the chief feature of the lakefront and the pinnacle of the 300 miles of dunes along the lake—stretching from here to the doorstep of Chicago.

Little Traverse Bay

Ten months out of every year they look like all the other small towns of the north, but in mid-June the wraps come off. Harbor Springs and Petoskey, on the opposite shores of Little Traverse Bay, emerge fresh as Cinderella in their costly summertime garb. Traffic picks up on the main streets. White sails dot the bay. The stores that boast "Palm Springs, Boca Raton, Petoskey" on their front doors reopen. The big spenders are back and all is right once more with Little Traverse Bay.

The area has always enjoyed the benefits of good publicity. The Ottawa regarded it as the most desirable of lands. Early reports from railroad men bubbled with enthusiasm. A Grand Rapids newspaperman visited on one of the first trains from the south and wrote glowing accounts of Petoskey's "million dollar sunsets." The railroads promoted excursions to the bay on their "Fishing Line" and told sportsmen that they weren't going to believe what they would catch here. Sprawling resort hotels rose along the bayshore.

About the turn of the century, the tourist phenomenon underwent a subtle change. Instead of staying in hotels, the wealthy visitors began building their own summer homes and settled in for the entire season—much as south Florida in recent years has changed over to condominium developments. With a droll *nostalgie de bouie*, the millionaires called their places cottages, although they could easily run to twenty rooms. They formed associations to guarantee the continued exclusivity of the developments. Land was not owned by individuals and could be resold only by the association. That kept out the riff-raff and just about anyone else the association members didn't care to live next to.

The most elaborate of the associations, Harbor Point, is closed to all automotive traffic; travel is restricted to horse and carriage. More accessible is the Wequetonsing Association. Several of its cottages are visible from Beach Road, east of Harbor Springs. In Bay View (the century-old Methodist summer camp), the grand old cottages painted in pastel shades can be seen along U.S. 31 north of Petoskey. The town is also the site of Stafford's Bay View Inn, one of the finest of the old resorts remaining in the area. Most of the others were either dismantled or burned after being deserted by the carriage trade.

Petoskey and Harbor Springs are 13 miles apart around the eastern end of the bay. For all purposes, though, they form one unit. Both have fine, public waterfront parks, extraordinary shopping, and a pair of little museums dedicated to their history. In Petoskey, the Little Traverse Regional Historic Society occupies the former Chesapeake and Ohio rail depot along the bayshore. There are exhibits dedicated to writers Ernest Hemingway and Bruce Catton, who both lived in the area, and a Victorian Room furnished with locally collected antiques. The star attraction, though, is the passenger pigeon. It is, of course, a stuffed pigeon. The birds, once so numerous that they darkened the skies over Petoskey, are now extinct and have been since World War I.

One of the early railroad promotional schemes involved hunting trips to the area. The game was passenger pigeons, which were regarded as a delicacy. There was really very little hunting involved. They were so plentiful that all one had to do was point his gun skyward and fire. While the wholesale slaughter of the pigeons was going on (literally millions were killed in a single season), something else was happening in the nearby forests. The nesting grounds of the birds were being destroyed by the massive lumbering operations. The pigeons could not overcome the resulting ecological imbalance, coupled with the wanton killing by hunters. In the space of a generation, the species was wiped out. Those who witnessed it wrote, in later years, that they still did not believe that such a thing could have happened. The birds seemed plentiful, as immune to change as the waters of the bay. But here in the museum is the stuffed pigeon; and even it is one of the few in existence. The museum is open from Memorial Day to Labor Day, Monday through Saturday, in the afternoons.

In Harbor Springs, the museum is dedicated to one of the village's leading pioneer residents, Andrew J. Blackbird. He was something of a Renaissance man, Ottawa style. Blackbird was a blacksmith, a silversmith, the postmaster, a historian of his nation, a teacher, and a government official. The museum on Main Street occupies what was his home and the post office. It houses exhibits on local tribal history and that of Harbor Springs. The Chief Blackbird Museum is open from 10:00 to 12:00 and 1:00 to 5:00 daily, from mid-June to Labor Day; free.

The Shay House next door is also worth a look. The hexagonal structure was built in 1888 by Ephraim Shay, locally famous as the inventor of a logging locomotive. The house now is occupied by a dress shop, which is more in keeping with the spirit of contemporary Harbor Springs.

The redevelopment of its business district won Harbor Springs an All-American City designation in 1975. The shops, extending along Main Street in a cluster of vintage structures, are weighted toward sportswear and unusual gifts. Even those who regard shopping as the next best thing to plague can appreciate the imagination and style that went into designing these shops. A turn to the left on any of the side streets will bring you to Bay Street and the waterfront. There is a park, a marina, and excellent views across the bay to Petoskey. Walk behind Holy Childhood Church at the head of Main Street, too, for a pleasant stroll through the town's shady square.

Petoskey is larger than tiny Harbor Springs and its shopping area, accordingly, is far more elaborate. Again the nineteenth-century facades have been utilized as much as possible, and the area is called the Gaslight District. It extends about one block in each direction from the intersection of Lake and Howard streets, adjacent to the town's main business district. There are outlets of nationally known stores here, along with strictly local operations and intriguing little complexes housing all sorts of unexpected shops. How can you resist a place called Toad Hall?

Best bet for a lunch stop while browsing is the Park Garden Cafe, just across the railroad tracks from the shopping district on Lake Street. It has been doing business at the same stand since 1879.

You may notice that in many shop windows there is jewelry featuring a highly polished, hexagonal stone that is divided into several nodules. This is the official state stone of Michigan, the Petoskey stone. One of the popular local diversions is searching for the stones along the beaches of Little Traverse Bay. They are not easy to find, of course, but make a handsome souvenir for those with a beachcombing inclination. The nodules were formed by skeletons of coral colonies that lived in the sea that covered this area some 300 million years ago.

Around Lake Charlevoix

The town bills itself as Charlevoix, the Beautiful, which may sound like the standard chamber of commerce hyperbole. In this case, however, the local drumbeaters are models of moderation. Charlevoix, both the town and the lake, are assuredly beautiful and perhaps even exquisite. There is a substantial body of opinion that together they compose the loveliest setting in Michigan's Lower Peninsula.

The harbor of Lake Charlevoix brings a lively boating panorama right into the middle of the town's business district. That district is concentrated on Bridge Street, the sole major avenue in town. One side is lined with flavorful shops and restaurants. On the other, a grassy park slopes down to the water's edge, where pleasure craft bob at anchor. The drawbridge that gives the street its name rises at intervals, permitting water traffic to pass through the channel dredged in the Pine River that connects Lake Michigan and Lake Charlevoix. The Weathervane Inn looms above on the channel bank, offering good meals in a delightful setting.

Rambling old homes overlook the lake from drives that skirt its edge. On its southern shore you can find smokehouses selling whitefish fresh from Lake Michigan. At the far end of the lake are public beaches. Just a few blocks west of the business district is still another broad beach fronting on Lake Michigan.

Lake Charlevoix itself is a double-armed body of water that cuts deeply into the rolling countryside. The area was settled heavily by Irishmen from Ulster who were moved to thoughts of home by the green hillsides. Echoes remain in a few names upon the land—the group of cities named Boyne and adjacent Antrim County. Beaver Island, a few miles off Charlevoix in Lake Michigan, remains a deeply Irish community. The broader branch of Lake Charlevoix extends about 12 miles southeast to its limit at Boyne City. The skinny, southern arm, in some places more like a river in appearance, ends at the sedate town of East Jordan. In either direction the scenery is delightful.

If you doubt the area's beauty, you will be disputing

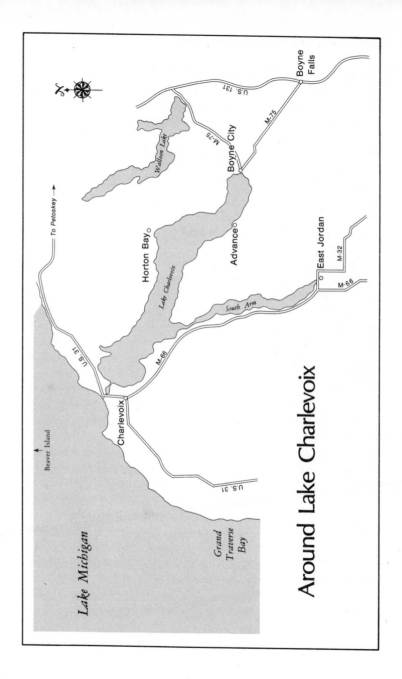

Around Lake Charlevoix

Ernest Hemingway, a man who knew fine scenery when he saw it. He spent his summers here as a young man at Horton Bay. The Hemingway family came from Oak Park, Illinois, and like many residents of the Chicago area they built a summer home in the Lake Charlevoix area. His sister, in fact, maintained the family residence there into the 1970s. Hemingway set one of his first short stories, "Up in Michigan," in Horton Bay. It was here that he married his first wife, Hadley Richardson, who figures so prominently in his autobiographical *A Moveable Feast*. Now it is a paltry saloon, indeed, in the lake area that doesn't claim Hemingway associations from his old summertime days.

Another Chicagoan who vacationed on the lake didn't turn out nearly so well. Richard Loeb's family lived a few miles south of Charlevoix. Just before the summer of 1924, Loeb and his friend Nathan Leopold kidnapped and murdered young Bobby Franks in one of the most notorious crimes of the century. The castle-like home built by Loeb's wealthy family is visible from Michigan 66. In the late 1970s, its ample grounds were being used for summer rock concerts.

A bit farther along Michigan 66 is the Ironton Ferry, an institution in this part of the country. The barge with a four-vehicle capacity—unless one of the vehicles turns out to be a camper—makes the crossing at the narrowest point of the lake's southern arm. By the time the toll of seventy-five cents has been collected from everyone, the ferry has reached the opposite side. Short as the crossing may be, it offers the quickest driving route from Charlevoix to Boyne City. If you're in no hurry, though, the drive along the southern arm of the lake is very pleasant, with views of the hills rising from the peninsula on the other shore. The town of East Jordan is a quiet resort favored by fishermen, and a flock of swans is usually visible on the lake near the outlet of the Jordan River.

Boyne City is the home of another miniature mode of transportation that is growing in popularity, the Boyne Valley Railroad. Unlike the Ironton Ferry, though, it serves no purpose whatsoever, aside from giving tourists a happy 14-mile round trip through hills and forests. The line leaves from the old depot in town for the short run to nearby Boyne Falls. Eventually, the operators hope to extend the line all the way to Petoskey— which still would be utterly without purpose, but an even happier ride. The route passes close to the Boyne Mountain ski resort, and an optional combination ticket is sold which includes both the rail trip and a ride on the Boyne ski lift for the view from the top. The train makes four daily round trips from Boyne City. It leaves every two hours between 10:00 and 4:00, from late June to Labor Day. There are weekend trips only from mid-May to mid-June and from Labor Day through mid-October.

Boyne City is also the center of a prolific mushroom area, and every May the city holds a competition to see who can pick the most in a ninety-minute period. Star attraction is the tasty morel, and the search for this delicacy usually attracts about three hundred contestants. Participants are led to the prime mushroom area and then turned loose with a sack to pick at will. Unregistered mushroom hunters can roam the hills as well to seek out the new crop.

The county road back to Charlevoix leads through Hemingway's Horton Bay and then through forested country on the sparsely settled northern shore. Antique stops can break up the trip for those with an eye for such things.

Sleeping Bear Dunes

The legend is almost as beautiful as the great dune itself. Once long ago, a forest fire broke out on the far Wisconsin shore of Lake Michigan. To escape the blaze, a mother bear and her two cubs leaped into the water and started to swim to the opposite side of the vast lake. The mother made it easily and lay down on the beach to await the arrival of her children, but the lake was very wide and they were very young. While still several miles offshore, they sank and were drowned. Manitou, the Great Spirit, taking pity on the mother bear, marked the spot of their sinking with an island, one for each of the cubs. Today they are North Manitou and South Manitou. The mother bear waits still, asleep on the beach, high atop the sand of the great Lake Michigan dunes.

The reality of the dunes' creation is, in geologic terms, a splendid tale as well. The ice covered this part of North America four times during the Pleistocene epoch, each time reshaping the contours of the land and preparing the way for the Great Lakes system. As the glaciers of the final ice age, the Wisconsin, re-treated north, they left behind the mineral matter that had been carried south with them on the advance from the Arctic. The material remained piled up in ridges and bluffs. One such bluff was left along the eastern shoreline of the body of water that would become Lake Michigan. On the beach far below, the prevailing west winds picked up the sand and began depositing it on the side of the bluff. After thousands of years, an eyeblink in geologic time, the bluffs were covered by the blowing sand and the great dunes that line the lakeshore had been formed.

Sleeping Bear, at 480 feet in height, is the greatest of them—a mountainous desert of restless inclination. The dunes move. They are alive. Geology did not end at the start of the twentieth century. The wind still blows and the sand continues to build. Sleeping Bear is known as the largest living sand dune in the world. It has covered parts of forests and even entire abandoned towns, uncovering them again years later. Just stand atop the dune, with the wind in your face and the sand blowing all about you, and you can sense the process working.

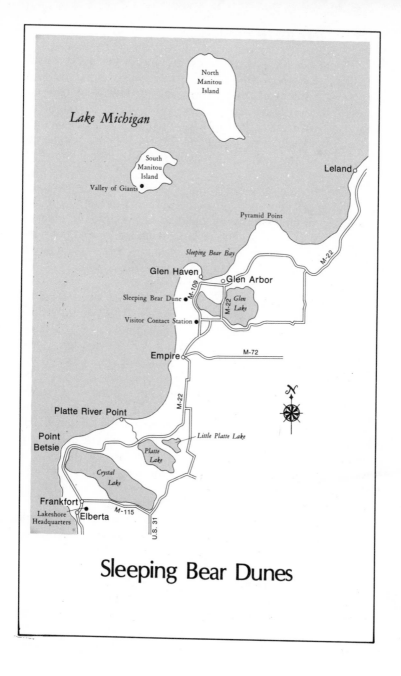

Sleeping Bear Dunes

There are three ways to see the top of the dunes in this National Lakeshore—by car, by dune wagon, and by foot. There is a toll road that enables you to drive your own car around the top of the dunes. The road is accessible off Michigan 109, just north of the park visitor station. It is a narrow strip, though, and it can be dangerous in wet weather because of skidding. At any rate, it is a way to see the dunes at your own pace.

The dune climb, a few hundred yards north of the toll road, is a thrilling excursion if you are hale. Teenagers can run up this mountain of sand effortlessly, but it's a little tougher for older or less fit folk to manage. The distance from the base to the summit is much longer than it looks; if you are not in the habit of exercising regularly, it will be a wheezing, arduous climb. There is no charge, however, for making it.

Then there are the dune wagon rides that leave regularly from the adjacent village of Glen Haven. The Warnes family has been operating these tours of the dunes since 1935 and now continue them under a National Park Service lease. The rides are a less strenuous way to travel the dunes, although the pace may be a little speedier than some would desire. The wagon, with oversize tires for traction through the sand, makes a looping circle around the dune with a number of viewing stops and a trip to the cluster of vegetation at the summit which makes up the "sleeping bear." The tours operate daily from 9:00 to 3:30 in June; from 9:00 to 5:30 in July and August. For the first part of September, tours operate every day except Monday, from 9:00 to 3:30; weekends only through mid-October with the same hours.

The area became a National Lakeshore in 1970 and is still in the process of being developed. A scenic parkway eventually will run along an inland ridge beyond the eastern border of the park and provide views across the dunes. It is still being designed. The acquisition of property for the park followed a lengthy and often acrimonious debate in the area between those favoring the park and property owners. About one-third of the eventual 60,000 acres has been acquired and many parcels of private land block access to Lake Michigan and inland points. Around the Sleeping Bear area, the best access is in Glen Haven—at the end of the road, past the dunes wagon concession. In the southern unit of the park there is an access road near Platte River Point.

A visitor station at the intersection of Michigan 22 and 109 has displays, maps, and information on the park. Aside from the dune, another interesting portion of the park includes Glen Lake, a hill-girdled jewel that is less than a mile from the advancing dunes. Splendid views across the water to the dunes open up from Michigan 22 as it crosses a narrow causeway just south of Glen Arbor. Another view from the heights, accessible a few miles along the Leelenau County road that branches off to the east, just past the causeway, is also impressive. You may continue the circuit of the lake through Burdickville on county roads. Canoe trips may be taken along the Platte River, in the southern portion of the park in Benzie County; information and rates are available at the Platte River Ranger Station.

The Manitou Islands are also part of the National Lakeshore. During the steamboat era, the islands were settled by woodcutters who harvested the forests and sold lumber to vessels that put in there. Today the islands are largely undeveloped, ideal vacation places for campers, hikers, and scuba divers. On South Manitou, the Valley of the Giants is a virgin, white cedar forest that escaped unscathed during the lumbering era. For back packers it is one of the most rewarding excursions in Michigan. Access to the islands can be made by regular boat service from Leland, about 20 miles north of Glen Arbor on Michigan 22. The boat leaves daily at 10 A.M. from June to Labor Day, returning to Leland at 5:00; on Sunday, it leaves at 1:00 and returns at 6:30. On Monday, Wednesday, and Friday, the boat stops first at North Manitou Island; on other days, it goes directly to South Manitou, giving you more time onshore during a one-day trip. In May and October the boats run on Monday, Wednesday, Friday, and the weekends, under the same schedules. Reservations may be made with Manitou Mail Service, Leland, Michigan. Boats may be chartered in Leland for diving trips, as well. There are also cottages available for summer rental on both islands.

Other Things to See

[1]   Cross Village was always a center of Indian life and, appropriately, it is now the site of the Great Lakes Indian Museum. The facility concentrates on the history and handiwork of the Ottawa and Chippewa, the two most prominent local tribes, with other displays given over to tribes also associated with Michigan. The museum, which also houses a crafts shop, is open daily from mid-June to Labor Day, 9:00 to 6:00; admission charge.

[2]   There is a vigorous school of thought that the most beautiful drive in Michigan is the course of Michigan 131 from Cross Village to Harbor Springs. The road plunges into dark forests, twists and turns along the lakeside bluffs, and tree trunks almost brush the side of your car as you pass. Unfortunately, there is only one stopping place for a view over the lake, just south of Good Hart, and the lake itself is obscured for most of the route by the thickness of the forest. It is, however, a trip with the feel of wooded depths to it. Watch for the turnoff to Middle Village and follow it for a look at the St. Ignatius mission church and Indian graveyard.

[3]   Beaver Island is the largest in Lake Michigan, a predominantly Irish community with vast sections of undeveloped forest land in its interior. There is little evidence remaining of its bizarre and often violent past when it was the site of a Mormon kingdom under the rule of Jesse Strang. He came here in 1847 after splitting from the main body of the church. While most of the group followed Brigham Young to Utah, an offshoot called the Order of Enoch gathered around Strang. It was a vaguely communistic system whose main thrust seemed to be the enrichment of Strang through the tithing system. Strang declared himself king and won control of the Charlevoix County government and legal system. In the resulting conflict with mainland gentiles, six of Strang's associates were killed in a gun battle over the selection of jurors. Strang eventually was assassinated in 1856 and the Mormons deserted the island. A museum in the former Mormon print shop in St. James, the island's lone settle-

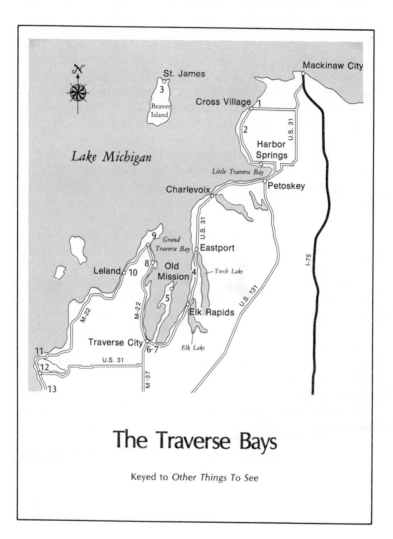

The Traverse Bays

Keyed to *Other Things To See*

ment, relates the history of the place. There is excellent hunting, fishing, swimming, and camping on the island, and the King Strang Hotel offers accommodations in St. James. One-day trips to the island with an optional guided bus tour can be made from Charlevoix, mid-June to Labor Day. The boat leaves from the harbor in Charlevoix. Schedules vary so it's best to call in advance to the Beaver Island Boat Company in Charlevoix, 616-547-2101.

[4]   From Eastport to Traverse City, U.S. 31 occupies a narrow ridge of land that runs between Lake Michigan and two large inland lakes, Torch and Elk. There is a pleasant roadside park just north of Elk Rapids, about midway on this 34-mile stretch.

[5]   The Old Mission Peninsula waves its finger into the midst of Grand Traverse Bay, neatly dividing it into two arms. The peninsula is covered with cherry orchards and driving up its central ridge in blossom time is an unforgettable way to welcome spring. Michigan 37 runs its entire length, starting a few miles east of downtown Traverse City and ending at the Old Mission Lighthouse on the forty-fifth parallel, midway between the equator and North Pole. The light is closed to the public but a footpath leads down to the water. At the town of Old Mission, a replica of the original mission church and the home of its pastor, built in 1842, stand along the water. On the return trip south, turn off Michigan 37 at Mapleton to the west and make the drive back to Traverse City along the Peninsula Drive. There are fine views of Marion Island and the Leelenau Peninsula across the bay. A good stopping place for a meal is the Bowers Harbor Inn.

[6]   Clinch Park is Traverse City's main recreational facility, featuring a marina, a zoo of animals found in Michigan, and the Con Foster Museum of Indian and pioneer relics. Admission is free to all attractions. The zoo is open from Memorial Day to mid-October, 9:30 A.M. to 10:00 P.M.; the rest of the year to 4:30. The museum is open from mid-May to Labor Day, 8:00 A.M. to 10 P.M. The museum's schedule for the rest of the year is weekdays, noon to 6:00; weekends, 10:00 to 6:00. The park is located on the West Bay off Grandview Parkway.

[7]   Downtown Traverse City's most interesting shopping area is a little tri-level complex called The Arcade, at 140 East Front Street. It has an assortment of pleasant specialty shops and a snack shop.

[8]   When the Reverend Peter Dougherty left the Old Mission Peninsula, he moved to Omena, across the bay on the Leelenau Peninsula. His lovely church there, built in 1858 after the New England model, houses the oldest Protestant congregation in northern Michigan.

[9]   Northport is a pleasant old town near the tip of the Leelenau Peninsula with several good antique stores. Peterson Park on Lake Michigan has blufftop views of the nearby islands and a good swimming beach.

[10]   Another Leelenau town with a distinct New England air to it is Leland. Its dock area has been turned into an evocative shopping district called Fishtown, with a variety of crafts and seafood stores housed in imaginative structures.

[11]   One of the most photogenic lighthouses in this part of the state is at Point Betsie, a few miles north of Frankfort on Michigan 22. It is one of the oldest, too, dating from 1858.

[12]   Frankfort is the terminus of the auto ferry that runs across Lake Michigan to Kewaunee and Manitowoc, Wisconsin. The sand dunes in the area are the yearly site of the National Hang Gliding and Soaring Festival. The event is usually held on the weekend before the Fourth of July.

[13]   One of the area's most breathtaking views of the lakeshore is about 10 miles south of Frankfort on Michigan 22; from a vantage point on a crest of the dunes, one can look down the coast in both directions.

Side Trips

Interlochen, 17 miles southwest of Traverse City, is the site of the National Music Camp, a summer program in the fine arts for gifted youngsters. There is instruction in music, dance, art, and drama. Visitors are encouraged to wander about the campus to watch rehearsals and attend the full program of concerts and recitals by students and visiting artists. During the winter months, Interlochen operates as an arts academy at the high school level. The concert calendar usually runs from late June to late August. Adult accommodations are available but should be reserved in advance from the camp. There is a charge for concert tickets.

The Platte River Hatchery, 20 miles east of Frankfort, produces about eight million Coho salmon, lake trout, and other varieties of game fish each year. Since the introduction of the Coho in these waters, the Platte has become one of the best fishing streams in Michigan. The hatchery is open daily. It is located on U.S. 31 east of Honor and it is free.

State Parks along Lakes Michigan and Charlevoix

Wilderness State Park—10 miles west of Mackinaw City on Emmet County roads, is a huge facility of 6,925 acres. Much of it has been turned over to a game preserve, and there is a naturalist, hunting in season, and cabins. Water-sports and picnicking facilities are also available along Waugoshance Point, the first Lake Michigan landfall west of the Strait of Mackinac. There are 210 campsites.

Petoskey—6 miles north of Petoskey on Michigan 131, has a beach on Little Traverse Bay and picnicking. There are 90 campsites.

Young—14 miles southwest of Charlevoix on county roads, adjoins the town of Boyne City on Lake Charlevoix. It has complete water facilities, picnicking, hiking trails, and 300 campsites.

Fisherman Island—12 miles south of Charlevoix, is a 2,500-acre lakefront facility opened in 1978. There is an excellent Lake Michigan beach, hiking trails, and outstanding hunting for Petoskey stones. There are 47 campsites.

Traverse City—2 miles east of Traverse City on U.S. 31, is a 39-acre facility with a beach on Grand Traverse Bay, fishing, and picnicking. There are 300 campsites.

Leelenau—7 miles north of Northport on a Leelenau County road, occupies a beautiful site at the top of the Leelenau Peninsula near the government lighthouse. The 460-acre site is being developed; there are now 42 campsites.

There are two camping areas in the Sleeping Bear National Lakeshore: D. H. Day, just east of Glen Haven, and Platte River, 11 miles northeast of Frankfort. Both are large areas with more than 2,000 acres of complete water-sports facilities.

The town of Holland—internationally famous for its Tulip Festival—is a successful example of how a rich, cultural heritage can be preserved in a modern community. *Courtesy Michigan Tourist Council.*

8

The Dutch and the Dunes

Think of the eastern Lake Michigan shoreline as a garden three hundred miles in length. Almost everything that doesn't require a tropical growing season will thrive here. Cherries from Traverse City, blueberries from South Haven, asparagus in Hart, and strawberries from Manistee. Apples and peaches grow in the endless orchards of Van Buren and Berrien counties, and grapes hang in the vineyards, making Michigan the third-leading state in the country in the production of wine.

The big lake to the west tempers the icy blasts that roll in from the plains in winter and moderates the summer heat. The Michigan lakeshore is buried in deeper snow each winter than any other nonmountainous area in the country. In the large cities like Grand Rapids and Muskegon, the result is frustration and highway tie-ups. But in the surrounding countryside, the earth lies protected beneath this deep, white shield. As a result, a northern location like Traverse City shows a more temperate yearly weather pattern than Chicago, a few hundred miles south but on the wrong side of the lake.

The same prevailing westerly winds that determine the area's weather also shaped its dominant physical feature—the

163

towering sand dunes that line the coast from Leelenau County to the doorstep of Chicago. As a result, the three-hundred-mile-long garden is fronted by a sand beach of the same length, one of the great water playgrounds in the country. The beach in the Grand Haven area, especially, is noted for its width and the gleaming whiteness of its sand. All along the shoreline there are major resort installations, with ten state parks in Michigan offering public access to these beaches and a National Lakeshore and state park along the dunes of Indiana.

This bountiful land attracted settlers as soon as western Michigan opened up in the 1830s and was one of the major destinations of the westward-bound immigrants who traveled the Erie Canal. They boarded ships in Buffalo, disembarked at Detroit, and struck out across the rolling Michigan countryside by foot and by wagon. The two most disparate groups that settled here were the Dutch and the House of David.

The Dutch came first, arriving in the area in 1846, just nine years after Michigan became a state. A group of religious dissenters, led by the Reverend Albertus Van Raalte, had abandoned their homeland earlier in the year and intended to begin a communal settlement somewhere in Wisconsin. By the time they reached Detroit, though, the long, snowy winter had settled in and the lake was closed for navigation. Governor Lewis Cass heard about the group of stranded immigrants and decided to assist them in finding land. Van Raalte and a small group of followers trudged through the deep snows to explore the shores of Black Lake, a few miles inland from Lake Michigan. Even in February he recognized the advantages of geography and climate in the location. "With many there was a faith in God and a consciousness of a noble purpose," he later explained. The religious colony was founded and became known as Holland. The city itself has become nationally famous for its Tulip Festival and Old World attractions. Its settlers, meanwhile, fanned out across the countryside so that Dutch remains the predominant ethnic influence in surrounding southwestern Michigan.

Benjamin Purnell brought his religious colony, the House of David, into the area about half a century later. The cult had been founded in England in 1792, and Purnell, a Kentuckian, joined the sect one century later in Detroit. After a split with the main American group, he moved to Benton Harbor with a company of seven followers in 1903. From this inauspicious start grew one of the strangest organizations the country has ever seen, exceeding even the renegade Mormon colony of "King" James Strang on Beaver Island (see chap. 7).

Purnell induced hundreds to join his colony on the condition that they surrender all their property to the group upon admission. Somehow, most of it wound up in the hands of Purnell. The settlement's agricultural enterprises prospered in the rich lands of Berrien County, but Purnell prospered even more. The House of David became a despotism, with policy decided at the whim of the leader. Purnell was a tremendous showman. He gained national attention with his bearded touring baseball team and later opened an amusement park on the grounds of the colony. Unfortunately, his sexual appetite was as voracious as his taste for wealth. Rumors of debaucheries leaked out of the House of David and a court order was obtained by the police to arrest Purnell in 1922. It took four years to find him, though, as his followers hid him within the grounds. Police finally arrested him in a surprise raid in 1926; he died a year later after being removed from control of the organization by the courts.

The House of David survived the episode and continues to be a going concern in Benton Harbor, welcoming visitors to the grounds during the summer months.

The biggest attraction in the area, however, is the wineries. Michigan trails only California and New York in American wine production, and in recent years the quality of the state wines has steadily improved. Two of the most consistent prizewinners in the state are Fenn Valley, near Fennville and south of Michigan 89 in Allegan County; and Tabor Hill, north of Buchanan in Berrien County. Both vineyards have tasting rooms, and visitors are welcome.

Holland

The Dutch came to western Michigan in 1846, fired by a quest for religious freedom and for land as rich as that they left behind in the Netherlands. They found both, and after three-quarters of a century, the tiny colony begun by the Reverend Albertus Van Raalte was a prosperous midwestern community. But many descendants of the settlers began to fear that something was being lost as well as gained. The original group had been persecuted by the established church in their homeland and were bound together by the experience, but the younger people seemed unaware of this heritage and uninterested in keeping it alive. Van Raalte had founded Hope College as a means of maintaining the original character of the settlement, but by the 1920s something more seemed to be needed.

Lida Rogus, a high school biology teacher in Holland, brooded about the problem. It finally occurred to her that the answer might be found in a flower. The tulip first appeared in the Netherlands in 1591, about thirty-five years after it had been introduced to Europe from Turkey. It thrived in the rich mucklands and became something of a national symbol. In a speech to the Holland Literary Club, Miss Rogus suggested that the symbol be transplanted from the old Holland to the new, as the focus of an ethnic festival. Her idea met with immediate acceptance and 250,000 tulip bulbs were imported from Europe in time to bloom in the spring of 1927. The event was Holland's first Tulip Festival.

Today the festival is the third best-attended event in the country, trailing only Mardi Gras in New Orleans and the Tournament of Roses in Pasadena. Hotels within a 50-mile radius of Holland are sold out a year in advance of the mid-May celebration. Films of the colorful flowers, the street-washing ritual, and klompen dancing in wooden shoes are familiar images all across North America.

Holland is more than a once-a-year attraction, however. Since the success of Miss Rogus's festival, there has been an ongoing effort to emphasize Holland's heritage. The town has two outstanding facilities dedicated to this concept: the Netherlands Museum, in the downtown area, and Windmill Island—a delightful park on the Black River. Other Dutch treats are scattered around the town. There are a couple of wooden shoe factories, a tulip garden, an amusement park-shopping plaza, and the campus of Hope College.

For an enjoyable tour of the area, start at the museum, at the corner of Central Avenue and Twelfth Street. It occupies a fine Victorian house built by one of Holland's early physicians and fronts on Centennial Park. The museum was a side benefit of the Tulip Festival. Historical displays were included in the 1937 festival and proved so popular that a permanent home was found for them here two years later. The museum is divided into three sections. On the top floor are exhibits relating to the old country. A highlight is the rooms furnished in the manner of the nineteenth-century town of Volendam and province of Zeeland. Many items are originals brought to America by immigrants from those places. A nearby town is, in fact, called Zeeland and was settled by people from that province. On the ground floor are exhibits on the history of Holland, Michigan, and in the basement are displays from the Dutch colonial possessions in the Pacific. The museum is open mid-May to mid-September, from 9:00 to 5:00; on Sundays, 11:30 to 5:00. There is an admission charge.

Cross the street for a brief stroll around Centennial Park, a beautifully landscaped square in the midst of the city. After a swing around the gardens, head east on Eleventh Street for one block. Across College Avenue is the impressive chapel of Hope College, built in 1929 in the Gothic style. The lovely, 170-foot-long nave is worth a visit inside. On the lawn at the entrance to the campus is an anchor, symbolizing the Reverend Van Raalte's naming of the college at its dedication in 1852: "This is my anchor of hope for this people in the future." It is a charming little school and its campus affords a delightful, leisurely stroll.

Return to your car and drive a few blocks east to Lincoln Avenue, then head north to reach the causeway to Windmill

Island. The centerpiece of this thirty-six-acre park is De Zwaan, an eighteenth-century windmill imported from Vinkel, in North Brabant. It was reassembled here, piece by piece, in 1964. Windmills are protected as national monuments in the Netherlands and generally not permitted to be altered or removed, but as a special token of the ties between the country and the Michigan city, the Dutch government located a suitable mill and permitted its export. It is believed to be the only authentic Dutch windmill in the United States.

Before exploring the park, stop in at the Post House near the parking area to see a film about the mill and how it was painstakingly transported to its new home. Then walk along the canal, cross the double drawbridge (a replica of one that crossed the Amstel River at Ouderkerk), and enter the mill. It is an enormous structure, the equivalent of a twelve-story building from base to top. You can climb to a platform just below the circling blades for a look across the park and the river. De Zwaan is still a working windmill, and two-pound bags of whole wheat flour ground here can be purchased in the park. Klompen dance exhibitions, put on during the summer by high school students, take place on the windmill's ground floor.

The park is splendidly landscaped. It is rounded out by a Dutch carousel and a miniature display called Little Netherlands—a tiny, mechanized panorama of the Dutch countryside within a group of buildings near the entrance. Although the park is not entirely free of commercial intrusions, they are kept to a minimum. In May and from July 1 to Labor Day, it is open from 9:00 to 6:00 on weekdays and 11:30 to 6:00 on Sundays. June hours are 10:00 to 5:00 during the week and 11:30 to 5:00 on Sunday. There is a single admission charge for all attractions.

Dutch Village is a less successful attempt to recreate the ambience of the old country. Within its rows of Dutch facades are shops, exhibits, klompen dancing, playgrounds, a Dutch amusement park swing, and a restaurant. It is located on U.S. 31 Bypass, north of Michigan 21. It is open daily from April to Labor Day, 9:00 to dusk; through mid-October it is open on

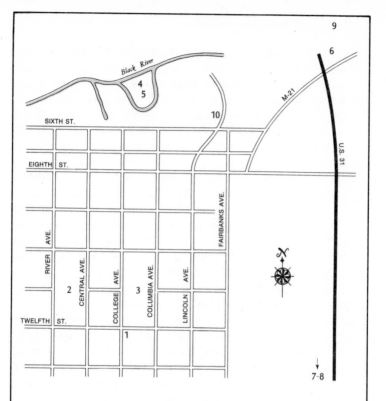

1 Netherlands Museum
2 Centennial Park Square
3 Hope College
4 Post House
5 Windmill Island
6 Dutch Village
7 Wooden Shoe Factory
8 DeKlomp Factory
9 Valdheer's Tulip Gardens
10 Baker Furniture Museum

Holland

weekdays to 4:30 and on weekends until 6:00. One admission charge covers all attractions.

Two places feature demonstrations of wooden shoe carving and the manufacture of Delftware. The DeKlomp factory is located on Thirty-Second Street, west of the U.S. 31 Bypass. It is open from May 1 to October 1, Monday through Saturday, 9:00 to 5:30; free. The slightly more elaborate Wooden Shoe Factory is located on the U.S. 31 Bypass near Sixteenth Street. It is open all year from 9:00 to 4:30, and from 8:00 to 4:30 in mid-May to mid-September. There is a small admission charge.

The biggest concentration of tulips in the area can be seen at Valdheer's Tulip Gardens, where one of the most diverse selections of bulbs in the country can be purchased. It is located on Quincy Street, north of the city and east of U.S. 31. The gardens are open all year; admission charge.

There is another place of interest in Holland that has nothing whatever to do with the Dutch; make an effort to see it anyhow. The Baker Furniture Museum is concerned with the staple product of the nearby community of Grand Rapids. This outstanding collection of antique pieces, assembled by furniture manufacturer Hollis Baker, was originally intended as a reference library for craftsmen studying old designs and attempting to make replicas. The museum was an afterthought, but this grouping of rooms by historic period is a delight (even for those who can't tell a Hepplewhite from a La-Z-Boy). The museum is located at East Sixth Street and Columbia Avenue. It is open from mid-May to mid-October, Monday to Saturday, 10:00 to 5:00; Sunday, 1:00 to 5:00. There is an admission charge.

Saugatuck

Artists fanned out from Chicago in the early years of the twentieth century to paint the scenery of the Midwest. One group wound up in the Rock River country of northern Illinois; another found its way to Brown County in the hills of southern Indiana; and a third settled amid the dunes and blue water of Saugatuck, Michigan.

This lakeshore village remains one of the oldest art colonies in the Midwest. Its Oxbow Summer School of Painting is an annual destination for students eager to spend their vacations in the study of art. The galleries along Butler Street are stocked with the work of students and their teachers. It isn't clear at this date who arrived here first, the artists or the tourists, but both groups remain interlocked in mutual support in Saugatuck.

The picturesque village along the Kalamazoo River grew up a mile or so inland from the lake. At the river's outlet is the lost city of Singapore, described by one writer as "Michigan's Pompeii." Singapore was a booming lumber town, abandoned when all the big trees were felled. Within a few years the relentless march of the sand dunes had completely covered the deserted town. Nothing remains to give a hint of what was there. A marker in front of the Saugatuck Village Hall commemorates Singapore; it will have to do until the dunes pass on and the buried town is uncovered once more.

The dunes also provide Saugatuck and its sister community of Douglas with excellent beaches. The Oval is regarded as the best, but visitors are tagged with a $1 parking fee on weekdays and $2 on weekends. Free beaches are situated in Douglas, at the foot of Center Street, and on Lakeshore Drive, five miles south of town. There are also dune schooner rides north of town on Sixty-Fourth Street. The twenty-two passenger vehicles cruise the dunes in the area of Goshorn Lake, an inland body of water cut off by the sand from Lake Michigan. They operate from 9:00 to 6:00 on weekdays and from noon to 6:00 on Sunday, May 1 to Labor Day.

Saugatuck's chief charms are right in the town itself: the

bright stores and galleries along Butler Street, the riverside park and the antique chain ferry that carries passengers across the Kalamazoo River, the historical museum, and the S.S. *Keewatin,* an even more fascinating floating museum that rests across the river in Douglas. It is the ideal, tranquil resort village. In half an hour you, yourself, may want to take up a brush and easel.

It wasn't always this way. There was a time in the 1950s and 1960s that Saugatuck had the unwanted reputation of being a northern Fort Lauderdale. During the summer months, vacationing collegians would use it as the base for beach and beer parties that sometimes turned into brawls amid the dunes. An ill-advised jazz and rock festival seemed to attract an even larger number of fun lovers who liked being rowdy in the sunshine. That era passed in the late sixties, though, and Saugatuck is again a village of artists.

Oxbow has been in operation since 1911, and the Taylor Art School has been open almost as long. Browse through the galleries and crafts shops along Butler and Water streets. Some specialize in leather, some in glass, and some in gold. One features homemade peanut butter in addition to enamel or copper birds—a little something for everybody. Sit for a while in the pleasant village square and then cut over to the river on Mary Street for a look at the chain ferry. This is a canopied, Victorian contraption operated by a hand-cranked chain. There is a toll. For a more extensive trip by water, there are cruises along the river and into the lake on the sidewheeler *Princess.* It leaves from the Lake Street dock at 1:00 and 7:30 for lake cruises and at 4:00 for a river jaunt. The boat is in operation from mid-June to Labor Day.

A nautical experience of a different kind can be found in Douglas, across the river where the old Great Lakes steamer *Keewatin* is berthed. The four-deck, 335-foot-long ship recalls a colorful vanished era on the Lakes. Once owned by Canadian Pacific Railroads, it carried passengers from Port McNichol on Georgian Bay through Sault Ste. Marie to Thunder Bay. It is a magnificent old vessel, still elegant even at rest. The fine, guided tour of the boat is like a short voyage back to the gilded age, complete with decorated glass and hanging plants on the promenade deck. The *Keewatin* is open daily from May to September, 10:00 to 4:30; admission charge.

The Saugatuck Historical Museum contains exhibits on the city's varied past and that of the vanished Singapore. It is located at 403 Lake Street and is open from noon to 4:30 every day except Saturday, when its hours are 10:00 to 4:30. There is an admission charge.

Indiana Dunes National Lakeshore

The most improbable thing about the Indiana Dunes is that the park exists at all. From its beaches you can see the skyline of Chicago across the southern end of Lake Michigan. On its western border is the Calumet District, one of the most intensively industrialized areas in the country. Motorists who drive through northern Indiana on the Toll Road and Chicago Skyway come away convinced that they have traversed a smoky, flaming nightmare where nothing of beauty can survive. But they are wrong.

The U.S. Steel Corporation carved the city of Gary from the dune country in 1906, naming it after its chairman of the board Elbert H. Gary. Along with the steel mills, oil refineries were built in the area. Then came chemical and cement plants. Before the creation of this mighty complex, the dune country had remained untouched and virtually uninhabited since it was formed by the last Ice Age, ten thousand years ago. Indian trails from Detroit to the west passed through the land. Pioneer accounts of travel through the area tell of wagons immobilized in the sand along the beaches and water lapping at the boots of travelers. A boat trip across the lake was much preferred to this uncomfortable, sandy trek, and so the dunes remained undisturbed.

After the founding of Gary, though, conservationists began to fear the spread of industry to the east might destroy this pocket of marsh and sand hills. An attempt to designate the area as a national park died out during World War I. Aided by contributions from Judge Gary and Chicago philanthropists, Indiana established a state park in the dunes in 1923.

After World War II, pressure built again for expanded industrialization and the building of a deep water port in the dune country. The plan appealed to the state of Indiana, which stood to gain thousands of jobs and substantial tax revenue from the projects. A group of local housewives, however, was horrified at the prospect and began a vigorous "Save the Dunes" campaign. They enlisted the support of powerful U.S. Senator Paul Douglas of Illinois and the National Lakeshore was created by

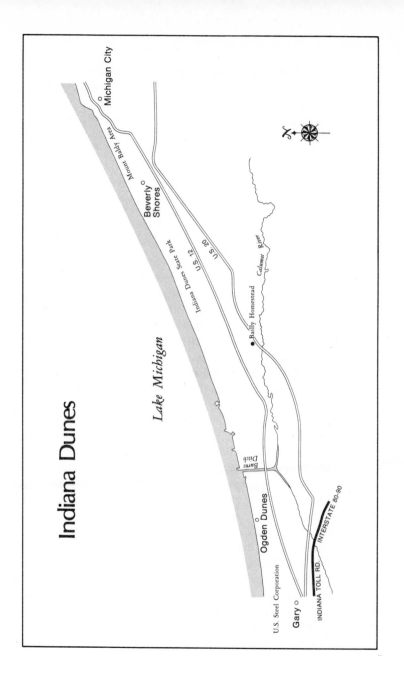

Indiana Dunes

Congress in 1966. Now encompassing 12,000 acres, the Lake-shore was the first urban national park and it halted the merci-less march of industry across the dunelands.

It is a rather patchwork arrangement. Much property re-mains in private hands and the separate areas of the park are not contiguous. In some cases whole communities are sur-rounded by federal land. There are five units in the Lakeshore, including the original state park still administered by Indiana. It is all somewhat confusing, but maps available at the visitor center will help sort things out. The center is located on U.S. 12, about 3 miles west of Michigan City and east of the state park entrance.

The park's perimeters also mark the birthplace of modern ecology. Dr. Henry C. Cowles, a pioneer in the field, was drawn to the dunes because of the consistent and fairly rapid change that occurs among plants in this environment. He studied the adaptability of plants and formulated landmark theories of plant distribution. The Cowles Bog is in the western area of the park. A 120-acre acid lake covered with vegetation, it is now a National Landmark. Tours are given by park rangers through the bog area. Check the visitor center for times.

The Lakeshore also clearly displays the three distinct kinds of dunes formed in this part of the country. Closest to the water are the foredunes, the highest and most recently formed. They are covered by only a thin layer of vegetation and are the most active since there is little to hold the sand in place when the winds blow. The highest dune in the park is Mount Baldy, just west of Michigan City; it is 135 feet high and may be climbed. Don't leave your car too long, though. The dune is moving south at the rate of four feet a year and one can see trees in the process of being buried by the sand near the parking area. The next dunes inland are the pine dunes, supporting not only that kind of tree but a great variety of grasses and shrubs, too. Fi-nally, stretching a mile or more away from the lake, are the oak dunes, looking more like forestland than dunes. They have been worn down so much over the centuries that they now can support towering trees.

Besides the natural areas of the Lakeshore, there is also a pioneer homestead being restored by the park service. The Bailly Homestead was built by a French-Canadian fur trader in the 1820s and was occupied by members of the family until 1917. Also on the grounds are a stagecoach tavern used on the Detroit-Chicago run, some workshops, and a chapel. The main house is not yet open to the public, but the family cemetery, south of U.S. 12 and west of Mineral Springs Road, is completely restored.

Another interesting area, although not actually part of the Lakeshore, is the resort of Beverly Shores. A few of the structures in town were moved here from the Chicago Century of Progress Exposition of 1933, including replicas of Boston's Old North Church and the Paul Revere House. Ask for directions at the Red Lantern Inn, the best hotel and restaurant in the immediate dunes area.

There are beaches in three areas of the park—West Beach, Mt. Baldy, and Indiana Dunes State Park—as well as in Beverly Shores. The park is open all year; the visitor center opens daily from 8:00 to 4:30. There is an admission charge to the Indiana State Park but not to the National Lakeshore.

Other Things to See

[1]   Manistee was once a rough and ready lumber town. It burned to the ground in 1871 and survived an even greater calamity in the next generation when the timber gave out. In recent years, Manistee has been restored to its full nineteenth-century luster by a Jaycee effort called Project Facelift. The entire downtown business district along River Street is now an attractive, bright area of vintage storefronts called Victorian Village. In its midst is the County Historical Museum, housed in an old general store, containing relics of the area's lively past. It is open daily from 10:00 to 5:00 except on Sundays and Mondays from November through April; free. Another civic museum is housed in the Water Works Building, on First Street near Cedar Street. It is open daily, 10:00 to 5:00, from June 1 to Labor Day except on Sundays; free. Excellent walking maps of the city's lumber-era mansions may be picked up at either museum.

[2]   Another proud relic of Manistee's past is the Ramsdell Opera House, built around 1900 by lumber baron T. J. Ramsdell. Generally not open for tours, the fine old theater presents stage productions from February through November. It is located on Maple and First streets. Inquire locally for show schedule.

[3]   Manistee National Forest sprawls over 497,000 acres south and east of Manistee. It is another of the reclaimed forests of the timber country. When established in 1938, the trees had been cut right down to the sand dunes. Now the land is again strong and green with many interior lakes, rivers for canoeing, and ski slopes. The headquarters is located in Cadillac. The forest also has an access area to Lake Michigan, south of the Mason County line and west of U.S. 31.

[4]   Father Jacques Marquette, his health failing, tried to return to his home mission of St. Ignace in 1675 after his exploration trip along the Mississippi River with Louis Joliet. But he only made it back as far as the site of Ludington before his condition worsened and he died. His companions buried him along a river near the lakeshore and two years later a party from

St. Ignace gathered the remains of the great explorer-missionary and returned them to the Straits of Mackinac for burial. A huge white cross atop a hill now marks the traditional spot of Marquette's first grave. It is located across the Pere Marquette River from downtown Ludington on Lake Shore Drive, west of U.S. 31 via Iris Road. Immediately south of the cross is Pioneer Village, a collection of historic structures from the environs of Mason County, including the first court house and a post office dating from 1850. The village is open from Memorial Day to Labor Day, 10:00 to 4:00; Sundays, 1:00 to 7:00; admission charge.

[5]   Ludington, unlike most other large cities in the area, fronts directly on Lake Michigan instead of being built along an interior river. Ludington Avenue, the town's attractive main street, dead ends right at the lake. There is car and passenger ferry service across the lake to Manitowoc and Milwaukee, Wisconsin, from early June to Labor Day. Check locally for time and rates.

[6]   Oceana County is asparagus country; on the second weekend of June each year there is a festival hailing the tasty vegetable in Hart, the county seat. They take the crop so seriously here that when a new highway was opened near Hart in 1975, instead of cutting a ceremonial ribbon they sliced a specially made chain of asparagus.

[7]   One of the finest scenic drives in this part of Michigan runs from Whitehall, along the shores of White Lake, through thick dark forests, down the dunes of Lake Michigan, and around the shores of Muskegon Lake to Muskegon. Follow South Shore Drive out of Whitehall until it becomes Scenic Drive. Then cut off north of Muskegon on Michigan 213.

[8]   Muskegon is another of the fabled old lumber towns that made the transition to the industrial age in good shape. It has built an enclosed shopping mall in the heart of downtown, but Muskegon is also preserving some of its picturesque past in the Heritage Village section, just west of downtown. Look in particular at the splendid old Hackley House, at West Webster Street and Sixth Street. Built by one of the pioneer timber bar-

ons, the house is open for tours on Wednesdays and weekends, 2:00 to 4:00. Just behind it on Clay Street, an old hose company has been turned into a firehouse museum. The Hackley Museum, one of the nicest small collections in the state, is located at 296 West Webster. It is open Monday to Saturday, 9:00 to 5:00; Sundays, 2:00 to 5:00; free.

[9]   Grand Haven's beach will sing to you when the wind is right. The fine grains of sand allegedly whistle in a recognizable musical note. As if that weren't enough, the resort also boasts the world's largest musical fountain. It's situated atop Dewey Hill, across the Grand River from the business district. Splashy concerts are given every evening; Memorial Day and June at 9:45, and the rest of the summer until Labor Day at 9:30. The fountain is 260 feet long and could fill 800 bathtubs to the depth of 12 inches with its water. The concerts are free of charge.

[10]   The area between Grand Haven and South Haven is rich in blueberry farms. South Haven, a lake resort in its own right, celebrates the crop with an annual festival in early July. Inquire locally for farms permitting pick-your-own berrying in the area.

[11]   The twin cities of Benton Harbor-St. Joseph were fortified by the French as early as 1679 when Robert LaSalle erected Fort Miami on the lake bluffs. The outpost was later moved to Niles, and the settlement at the outlet of the St. Joseph River split in two. Benton Harbor became a commercial center, St. Joseph a resort. The two combine to celebrate the Blossomtime Festival each May, a tribute to the surrounding orchard lands. A continuing tribute of sorts takes place at the Benton Harbor Fruit Market, the largest noncitrus grower's market in the world. Located at 1891 Territorial Road, it operates daily from 9:00 to noon, June to October. The site of Fort Miami is marked with a historic plaque in downtown St. Joseph, at Lake Boulevard and Ship Street.

[12]   An especially lucid explanation of nuclear power is available at the Donald C. Cook Nuclear Power Plant, just north of Bridgman. The entrance is on U.S. 31. The visitor

Eastern Shore of Lake Michigan

Keyed to *Other Things To See*

center is open Wednesday to Saturday, 10:00 to 6:00; Sundays, noon to 6:00. Opening times are one hour earlier from June to early September. There is no admission charge.

[13]   One of Michigan's wineries is situated right off the lake. It is called, appropriately enough, Lakeside Vineyard. Located in Harbert, just off Interstate 94, it offers a guided tour of the winery and a visit to the tasting room. The winery is open mid-April through December from 9:30 to 4:00, Monday to Saturday; 12:30 to 5:00, Sunday.

[14]   Both Harbert and Sawyer are heavily Swedish in their makeup, settled by emigrants from the Chicago area. Watch for the Swedish bakeries along U.S. 31.

[15]   Michigan City's pride is Washington Park, a 90-acre lakefront facility with beaches, a marina, a zoo, and a museum in Indiana's oldest lighthouse. On the weekends there is a parking fee for nonresidents. The zoo is open from 10:00 to 8:00, May through Labor Day; to 4:00 the rest of the year. There is an admission charge. The lighthouse, built in 1858, is open every day except Monday from 1:00 to 4:00; admission charge.

[16]   One of the most ornate Victorian mansions in the Midwest open to the public is Michigan City's Barker House. A thirty-eight room home built in 1905 by a railroad magnate, the mansion now is owned by the city and is used as a civic center. The opening times vary widely and it is best to call ahead to set up a guided tour. The number is 219-872-0159. It is located on Washington Street and Seventh Street.

Side Trips

Grand Rapids, 35 miles east of Grand Haven, is Michigan's second largest city and famous nationally as a furniture manufacturing center. The striking Alexander Calder sculpture *La Grande Vitesse* in the plaza of Vandenbergh Center is the focal point of the redeveloped downtown area. Another crowd-pleasing addition to the area is the fish ladders at the Sixth Street dam, where Coho salmon work their way upstream. The city has two excellent museums. The Art Museum, at 230 East Fulton Street, with a fine German Expressionism collection, is free and open from 9:00 to 5:00, Monday to Saturday; 2:00 to 5:00 on Sunday; closed Mondays in summer. The Public Museum, at 54 Jefferson Avenue S.E., has exhibits on the history of furniture and the city. It is also free and open 10:00 to 5:00 weekdays; 2:00 to 5:00 weekends.

Paw Paw, 33 miles northeast of Benton Harbor, is the center of Michigan's wine industry. Four wineries in a 20-mile radius of town offer tours and tasting. Frontenac, Warner, and St. Julian are located in Paw Paw, while the Bronte winery is in Keeler, about halfway between the town and Benton Harbor. For other vineyards in the area see the introduction to this chapter and Other Things to See.

Niles, 24 miles southeast of St. Joseph, was the site of Fort St. Joseph, a major outpost of the French from 1720 to 1763. It fell to the Indians after the British takeover in Pontiac's Rebellion and was never rebuilt. A Spanish force out of St. Louis captured the site for a day in 1781, the only action during the revolutionary war in Michigan. A museum at Fifth and Main streets houses relics of the fort. It is open Tuesday to Sunday, 1:00 to 5:00; free.

South Bend, 34 miles east of Michigan City, is the home of the University of Notre Dame, one of the country's most famous institutes of higher learning. Tours of the lovely campus are available during the summer months from 9:00 to 5:00 and can be arranged by calling the university's information service at 219–283–7367.

State Parks along the Lake

Orchard Beach—3 miles north of Manistee on Michigan 110, is set on a bluff above the lake with a beach and picnic facilities. There are 175 campsites.

Ludington—8 miles north of Ludington on Michigan 116, is a sprawling 4,156-acre facility with complete water-sports facilities on Lake Michigan, Lake Hamlin, and the Big Sable River. It also has a good system of nature trails. There are 398 campsites.

Mears—14 miles south of Ludington on U.S. 31, has an

excellent sand beach and picnic and water-sports facilities; 179 campsites.

Silver Lake—10 miles west of Hart on Oceana County Road B 15, has beaches on an inland lake that is separated from Lake Michigan by towering sand dunes. A concession in the park offers rides over the sand. There are 249 campsites.

Muskegon—6 miles west of Muskegon on Michigan 213, has water sports and a replica of a frontier blockhouse with views down the dunes. There are 357 campsites.

Hoffmaster—just north of Grand Haven on U.S. 31, has beaches and water-sports facilities amid the dunes and woods. There are 333 campsites.

Grand Haven—just south of the town's business district, is one of the finest beaches in the state; 170 campsites.

Holland—7 miles west of Holland on county roads, has good beaches in the dunes, perch fishing, and 342 campsites.

Van Buren—2 miles south of South Haven, has a beach, water sports, and towering dunes. There are 197 campsites.

Warren Dunes—15 miles south of St. Joseph, is an especially nice beach area backed by dramatic dune country; 249 campsites.

Indiana Dunes—10 miles west of Michigan City, is discussed on p. 174. There are 315 campsites.

Bibliography

Adams, John R. *Harriet Beecher Stowe*. New York: Twayne Publishers, 1963.

Bald, F. Clever. *Michigan in Four Centuries*. New York: Harper and Row, 1954.

Barcus, Frank. *Freshwater Fury*. Detroit: Wayne State University Press, 1960.

Barry, James P. *Georgian Bay*. Toronto: Clarke, Irwin & Co., 1968.

Bayliss, Joseph and Estelle. *Historic St. Joseph Island*. Cedar Rapids: Torch Press, 1938.

Beers, Henry Putney. *The French and British in the Old Northwest*. Detroit: Wayne State University Press. 1964

Boyer, Dwight. *True Tales of the Great Lakes*. New York: Dodd, Mead & Co., 1971.

Brebner, J. Bartlet. *Canada: A Modern History*. Ann Arbor: University of Michigan Press, 1970.

Brown, Prentiss M. *The Mackinac Bridge Story*. Detroit: Wayne State University Press, 1956.

Brown, Robert Benaway. *The Netherlands and America*. Ann Arbor: University of Michigan Press, 1947.

Channing, Edward. *The Story of the Great Lakes*. New York: Macmillan, 1912.

Conot, Robert. *American Odyssey*. New York: William Morrow & Co., 1974.

Curwood, James Oliver. *The Great Lakes*. New York: G. P. Putnam's Sons, 1909.

Fox, William S. *The Bruce Beckons*. Toronto: University of Toronto Press, 1952.

Gynin, Brion. *To Master—a Long Goodnight*. New York: Creative Age Press, 1946.

Hatcher, Harlan H. *The Great Lakes*. New York: Oxford University Press, 1944.

——. *Lake Erie*. New York: Bobbs-Merrill, 1945.

Havighurst, Walter. *The Long Ships Passing*. New York: Macmillan, 1953.

——. *Three Flags at the Straits*. Englewood Cliffs: Prentice-Hall, 1966.

Holbrook, Stewart H. *Holy Old Mackinaw*. New York: Macmillan, 1938.

Hough, Jack L. *Geology of the Great Lakes.* Champaign: University of Illinois Press, 1958.

Inland Seas. Quarterly Journal of the Great Lakes Historical Society, Cleveland.

Landon, Fred. *Lake Huron.* Indianapolis: Bobbs-Merrill, 1944.

LeBaudais, D.M. *Sudbury Basin.* Toronto: Ryerson Press, 1953.

Malkus, Alida. *Blue-Water Boundary.* New York: Hastings House, 1960.

May, George Smith. *The Forts of Mackinac.* Mackinac Island State Park Commission, 1962.

Michigan: A Guide to the Wolverine State. New York: Oxford University Press, 1956.

Michigan History. Magazine of the Michigan Historical Commission, Lansing.

McKee, Russell. *Great Lakes Country.* New York: Crowell, 1966.

Putnam, Donald F. *A Regional Geography of Canada.* Toronto: M. Dent and Sons, 1956.

Quaife, Milo M. *Lake Michigan.* Indianapolis: Bobbs-Merrill, 1944.

Ratigan, William, *Straits of Mackinac.* Grand Rapids: Eerdmans, 1957.

Rourke, Constance Mayfield. *Trumpets of Jubilee.* New York: Harcourt, Brace & Co., 1927.

Steinman, David B. *Miracle Bridge at Mackinac.* Grand Rapids: Eerdmans, 1957.

Index

187

Conversion Chart

Because the metric system is presently in use in Canada and because the United States is in the process of converting to the metric system, the following chart is provided for your convenience.

1 inch = 2.54 centimeters
1 foot = 0.304 meters
1 mile = 1.6 kilometers
1 square mile = 2.59 square kilometers
1 acre = 0.405 hectares
1 gallon = 3.75 liters